A Canadian Walks Into a Bar...

One-liners, Two-liners, Humorous Stories, Quips, Jibes & Hilarious Stuff

David MacLennan

FOLK
LORE
PUBLISHING

©2013 by Folklore Publishing
First printed in 2013 10 9 8 7 6 5 4 3 2 1
Printed in Canada

All rights reserved. No part of this work covered by the copyrights hereon may be reproduced or used in any form or by any means—graphic, electronic or mechanical—without the prior written permission of the publisher, except for reviewers, who may quote brief passages. Any request for photocopying, recording, taping or storage on information retrieval systems of any part of this work shall be directed in writing to the publisher.

The Publisher: Folklore Publishing
Website: www.folklorepublishing.com

Library and Archives Canada Cataloguing in Publication

MacLennan, David, 1977–
    A Canadian walks into a bar— / David MacLennan.

ISBN 978-1-926677-88-0

1. Canadian wit and humor (English).2. Canada—Humor. 3. National characteristics, Canadian—Humor. I. Title.

PN6178.C3M26 2013   C818'.602   C2012-908202-3

Project Director: Faye Boer
Project Editor: Kathy van Denderen
Cover Image: Cover illustration by Roger Garcia

We acknowledge the support of the Alberta Multimedia **Government** Development Program for our publishing program. **of Alberta** ■

We acknowledge the financial support of the Government of Canada through the Canada Book Fund (CBF) for our publishing activities.

  Canadian   Patrimoine
         Heritage   canadien

PC: 1

⋉ CONTENTS ⋊

✎ Introduction ✎

We Canadians are a strange lot. We're all welcoming and nice on the outside, but on the inside, we are an odd assortment of characters that collectively have a weird sense of humour that is recognized worldwide. Heck, why do you think so many Canadian comedians and writers live in Hollywood? I believe it's because Canadians understand that a joke is a joke, and that life is more enjoyable when you can laugh at yourself. If this weren't true, the Newfies would have separated from Canada a long time ago. So be prepared to have a good laugh at yourself while reading this book.

I have tried to compile a wide variety of jokes about stereotypical Canadians of course—like the hoser and the hockey player—but I have also added many jokes of modern Canadians going about their days, like an old man going to the doctor or a Montréal kid in school. And don't be fooled by how light some of these jokes may sound. This collection also contains a few dirty, crude and sometimes blue jokes, because in truth, only the really best jokes will make you grimace and say, "OMG!"

There are hundreds of funny jokes, stories, puns and one-liners that poke fun at just about every region, province, language and stereotype in this vast frozen country of ours. If I have left anyone out, I apologize, but trust me, I'll get you next time.

Now, just sit back, relax (I'm sure at least one of you is reading this on the john, so really relax) and I guarantee you will laugh your way through each page of this book. Share these jokes with your friends, your co-workers, and if you're feeling adventurous, tell them to your ultra-religious aunt. I promise you will get everyone laughing. If they don't, then they ain't *Canadian*!

⋘ CHAPTER ONE ⋙

A Canadian Walks into a Bar

One Too Many

A Russian, a Frenchman and a Canadian walk into a bar. The Russian asks the bartender for vodka, so he gives him an entire bottle. The Russian pours out a shot, drinks it and throws the rest of the bottle into the air and shoots it.

The bartender asks, "What did you do that for?"

The Russian replies, "In my country, we have too much vodka."

The bartender shakes his head and turns to the Frenchman, who orders wine. The Frenchman pours a glass, drinks it, then throws the rest of the bottle in the air and shoots it to smithereens. "In my country," he says, "we have too much wine."

The bartender shakes his head again, and turns hesitantly to the Canadian to ask him what he would like.

The Canadian orders a beer, drinks the whole bottle in one go, then pulls out his gun and shoots the Frenchman. "In my country," he says, "we have too many Frenchmen."

In a Newfie Bar

A guy walks into a bar and sees a dog lying in the corner licking his balls. He turns to the bartender and says, "Boy, I wish I could do that."

The bartender replies, "You might want to pet him first."

A Stranger in a Bar

A guy walks into a bar in northern Alberta and asks the bartender, "Hey, you hear the latest Canadian joke?"

The bartender says, "Hey, pal, before you start, you see those two lumberjacks fighting in the corner? You see the big hockey players behind you? You see that hunter next to you at the bar, and the fisherman next to him? You see me? We're all Canadian. You still want to tell your little joke?"

Q: How can you tell if there's a drunk Newfie in the hospital?

A: He's the person blowing the foam off the bedpans.

The guy looks around at all the bruisers in the bar, who have now started to pay attention to him. "Yeah, okay," the guy says, "I'll tell it slow.

That's My Boy

A Canadian guy is drinking in a New York bar when he gets a call on his cellphone. After he's done with the call, he starts grinning from ear to ear and orders a round of drinks for everybody in the bar because, he announces, his wife has just delivered a typical Canadian baby boy weighing 25 pounds.

Nobody can believe that any newborn can weigh 25 pounds, but the Canuck just shrugs and says, "That's about average up North, folks. Like I said, my boy's a typical Canadian baby boy."

Congratulations are showered upon him from everyone in the bar. One woman actually faints because of sympathy pains.

Two weeks later, the Canadian father returns to the bar.

The bartender says, "Say, you're the father of that typical Canadian baby that weighed 25 pounds at birth, aren't you? Everybody has been makin' bets about how big he'd be in two weeks. We were gonna call you. So how much does he weigh now?"

The proud father answers, "Seventeen pounds."

The bartender is puzzled and concerned. "What happened?" he asks. "He already weighed 25 pounds the day he was born."

The Canadian father takes a long swig from his beer, wipes his lips on his shirtsleeve, leans toward the bartender and proudly says, "Had him circumcised."

In a Regina Bar

"Shhaaayyy, buddy, what's a 'Breathalyzer'?" asks one drunk to his friend at the next bar stool.

"Well, I'd have to say it's a bag that tells you when you've drunk way too much," replies the equally wasted gent.

"Ah hell, whaddya know? I've been married to one of those for 10 years now!"

Seal Drinker

A seal walks, or rather waddles, into a bar and asks the bartender for a drink.

The bartender asks the seal, "What's your pleasure?"

The seal replies, "Anything but Canadian Club."

Designated Driver

Late one night, a police vehicle is parked outside a popular Montréal tavern. After last call, the police officer notices a man leaving the bar so intoxicated that he can barely walk. The man stumbles around the street for a few minutes, with the officer quietly observing. After what seems an eternity and trying his keys on five different vehicles, the man finally manages to find his car, which he subsequently falls into. He stands there for a few minutes as a number of other patrons leave the bar and drive off.

> Q: What's the difference between an American and a Canadian?
>
> A: A Canadian not only has a sense of humour but can also spell it.

Finally the man starts the car, switches the wipers on and off (it was a fine dry night), flicks the blinkers on, then off, honks the horn and then switches on the headlights. The drunk man then moves the vehicle forward a few feet, reverses a little and then remains still for a few more minutes as more vehicles leave the establishment. At last he pulls out of the parking lot and starts to drive slowly down the road.

The police officer, having patiently waited all this time, now starts up his patrol car, puts on the flashing lights and promptly pulls the man over and carries out a Breathalyzer test. To his amazement, the Breathalyzer indicates no evidence that the man has consumed any alcohol at all.

Dumbfounded, the officer says, "I'll have to ask you to accompany me to the police station. This Breathalyzer equipment must be broken."

"I doubt it," replies the man, smiling. "Tonight I'm the designated decoy."

Dirty Thief

An Englishman, an American and a Canadian are sitting in an airport lounge. They each buy a pint of beer. Just as they are about to enjoy their tasty beverages, a fly lands in each of their pints.

The Englishman pushes his beer away from him in disgust.

The American fishes the offending fly out of his beer and continues drinking it as if nothing happened.

The Canadian picks the fly out of his drink and starts shaking it over the pint, yelling, "Spit it out! Spit it out, you bastard!"

Battle of Wits

While sitting in a bar, Ken, a Torontonian, and Barry, a Newfie, get into an argument about who is smarter. After much arguing back and forth, the two decide that the only way to solve the problem is for them to do a quiz.

Ken confidently lays out the rules. If Barry cannot answer any of Ken's questions, Barry will have to hand over $5, but if Ken cannot answer then he will give Barry $50. Barry accepts the bet.

Ken asks the first question: "What is the largest planet in the solar system?"

Barry thinks for a moment but comes up with nothing and is therefore obliged to hand over $5.

Now, it is Barry's turn. He thinks for a moment, then asks, "What climbs up a hill on four legs but climbs down on three?"

Ken accepts the challenge. He racks his brain for over 20 minutes but can come up with no suitable answer to fit the Newfie's question. Ken can hardly believe that a Newfie has bested him in a game of wits, but he reluctantly concedes defeat and pulls out a $50 bill and slides it over to Barry.

Ken then asks, "I have to know the answer. Please tell me. What climbs down on three legs?"

Barry thinks for a moment, puts his hand in his pocket and hands over $5.

Visualization Method

A Montréaler walks out of a bar on Crescent Street, stumbling back and forth with a key in his hand. A cop on the beat sees him and approaches.

"Can I help you, sir?" the cop asks.

"Yessh! Sshomebody sshtole my car!" the man replies.

The cop asks, "Where was your car the last time you saw it?"

"It wasssh at the end of thissssh key!" the man replies, logically, if a bit too literally.

About this time the cop looks down to see that the man's weenie is being exhibited for the entire world to see. He asks the man, "Sir, are you aware that you are exposing yourself?"

The man looks down woefully and without missing a beat, moans, "Oh, no! They got my girl-friend too!"

Pull Over

A drunk is driving through Toronto, and his car is weaving violently all over the road. A cop pulls him over and asks, "Where have you been?"

"I've been to the pub," slurs the drunk.

"Well," says the cop, "it looks like you've had quite a few."

"I did all right," the drunk says with a smile.

"Did you know," says the cop, standing straight and folding his arms, "that a few intersections back, your wife fell out of your car?"

"Oh, thank heavens," the drunk says with relief. "For a minute there, I thought I'd gone deaf."

Frog

A Quebecker walks into a pub with a frog on his head.

The bar attendant asks, "What's that on your head?"

The frog says, "I don't know, but it started out as a wart on my bum!"

Shy Guy

A polite but shy guy from Kelowna goes into a bar and sees a beautiful woman. After an hour of gathering up his courage, he finally goes over to her and asks, tentatively, "Um, would you mind if I chatted with you for a while?"

She responds by yelling at the top of her lungs, "No, I won't sleep with you tonight!"

Everyone in the bar is now staring at them. Naturally, the guy is hopelessly and completely embarrassed, and he slinks back to his table.

After a few minutes, the woman walks over to him and apologizes. She smiles at him and says, "I'm sorry if I embarrassed you. You see, I'm a graduate student in psychology, and I'm studying how people respond to embarrassing situations."

To which he responds, at the top of his lungs, "What do you mean $200?!"

Bar Talk

A bored guy sitting in a bar is looking to strike up a conversation. He turns to the bartender and says, "Hey, about those NDPs in Parliament..."

"Stop right there, pal—I don't allow talk about politics in my bar!" interrupts the bartender.

A few minutes later, the guy tries again. "People say about the Pope that..."

"No religion talk, either," the bartender cuts in.

The guy tries one more time to break the boredom. "I thought the Leafs would..."

"No sports talk. That's how fights start in bars!" the barman says.

"How about sex? Can I talk to you about sex?"

"Sure. That we can talk about," replies the barkeep.

"Great! Go screw yourself!"

Q: What do urine samples and Canadian beer have in common?

A: The taste!

Stranger

A guy walks into a bar in rural Alberta and orders a glass of white wine. Everybody sitting around the bar looks up, expecting to see some pitiful Toronto queer.

The bartender looks up and says, "You ain't from around here, eh? Where ya from, eh?"

The guy says, "I'm from Vernon."

The bartender replies, "What the heck do you do in Vernon?"

The guy replies, "I'm a taxidermist."

The bartender says, "Now just what the heck is a taxidermist?"

"I mount animals," the guys says nervously.

The bartender grins and shouts out to the whole bar, "It's okay, boys! He's one of us!"

Hard Drinker

A Newfie has been drinking at a pub all night. The bartender finally tells him that the bar is closing. The Newfie stands up to leave and falls flat on his face. He tries to stand one more time; same result. He figures he'll crawl outside and get some fresh air, and maybe that will sober him up.

Once outside, he stands up and again falls flat on his face. He decides to crawl the four blocks home. When he arrives at the front door, he stands up, opens the door and again falls flat on his face. He crawls into his bedroom.

When he reaches his bed, he tries one more time to stand up. This time he manages to pull himself upright, but he quickly flops right into bed and is sound asleep as soon as his head hits the pillow.

He awakens the next morning to his wife standing over him, shouting, "So, you've been out drinking again!"

"What makes you say that?" he asks, putting on an innocent look.

"The pub called; you left your wheelchair there again."

Amazing!

A guy walks into a bar in Regina and asks the bartender if he will give him a free beer if he shows him something amazing.

The bartender agrees, so the guys pulls out a hamster that begins dancing and singing "Courage" by the Tragically Hip.

"That *is* amazing!" says the bartender and gives the guy a free beer.

"If I show you something else amazing, will you give me another free beer?"

The bartender agrees, so the guy pulls out a small piano and a frog.

Now the hamster plays the piano while the frog dances and sings "Summer of '69" by Bryan Adams.

The bartender, completely wowed, gives the guy another beer. A man in a suit, who's been watching the entire time, offers to buy the frog for a princely sum, which the man agrees to.

"Are you nuts?" says the bartender to the man with the hamster. "You could've made a fortune off that hamster."

"Can you keep a secret?" says the man. "The hamster is a ventriloquist."

Little Guy

A guy walks into a bar in Winnipeg. He has a fat wallet in his pocket, two beautiful blondes on either arm and a little man on his shoulder.

The bartender thinks this is odd but figures it would be okay to serve him.

The guy asks if he can buy everyone in the house a drink. The bartender looks at him kinda funny and says, "Sir, I'm gonna have to see some money before I can pour that many drinks." The guy reaches into his wallet, pulls out a bunch of $100 bills and lays five of them on the bar.

The bartender pours all the drinks, and just as he has finished pouring the last one, the little man on the rich guy's shoulder runs down his arm, hops off his hand and knocks every drink over then proceeds back up the man's arm.

The man tells the bartender he wants to order everyone in the house a drink. The same exact thing happens again.

For the third time, the man asks to buy the house a round.

The bartender looks at the guy and says, "Brother, do you not realize what is happening here? I can't keep pouring these drinks. Now, what is the deal?"

The man sighs and says, "Well, one day I was walking along the beach when I found a bottle. A genie popped out and said he could grant me three wishes. The first thing I wished for was a wad of $100 bills that never ended. Next I wished for two gorgeous blondes to have for the rest of my life."

The bartender says, "Well, what was the third thing you wished for?"

The man replies, "A 12-inch prick."

Home Country

A Newfie is sitting in a bar when he spots a pretty young woman. He starts to walk toward her when the bartender says to him, "Don't waste your time on that one. She's a lesbian."

The Newfie goes over to her anyway and says, "So which part of Lesbia are you from?"

> **Q:** What is the one thing that all men at Calgary single bars have in common?
>
> **A:** They are all married.

Up North Bar

A drunk man is wandering around the parking lot of a local bar in Yellowknife. He bumps into vehicles and starts rubbing the roofs of the cars.

The manager comes out of the bar and stops the guy.

"What the heck are you doing?" he asks the drunk.

"I'm looking for my car, and I can't find it," replies the drunk.

"So how does feeling the roof help you?" asks the puzzled manager.

"Well," replies the drunk earnestly, "my car has two blue lights and a siren on the roof!"

Sold

A drunk walks into a bar crying in Halifax. One of the other men in the bar asks him what happened.

"I did a terrible thing," sniffs the drunk. "Just a few hours ago I sold my wife to someone for a bottle of Canadian Club."

"That is awful," says the other guy. "And now that she is gone you want her back, right?"

"Right!" says the drunk, still crying.

"You're sorry you sold her because you realized too late that you still loved her, right?"

"Oh, no," replies the drunk. "I want her back because I'm thirsty again!"

Screech!

Three Newfie women leave separately after a very late night out drinking Screech until the early hours. They meet the next afternoon for a pint and compare notes about who had been the most drunk.

The first gal claims that she was the drunkest, saying, "I drove straight home, walked into the house and as soon as I got through the door, I blew chunks."

To which the second gal replies, "You think that was drunk? I got in my car, drove out of the parking lot and wrapped my car around the first tree I saw. I don't even have insurance!"

And the third woman proclaims, "I was by far the most drunk. When I got home, I got into a big fight with my husband, knocked a candle over and burned the whole house down!"

The women all look at each other for a moment and then the first gal says, "Ladies, I don't think you understand. Chunks is my dog."

Food and Drink

A sandwich walks into a bar. The barman says, "Sorry, we don't serve food in here."

Smart Lawyer

A Calgary lawyer is sitting in a bar having a drink when a beautiful woman sits down next to him. The lawyer, seeing an opportunity, buys the woman a martini and proceeds to hit on her. He then asks her, "Would you sleep with me for a million dollars?"

The woman looks at him and says, "You know, for a million dollars, sure."

The lawyer then asks, "Would you sleep with me for 20 dollars?"

The woman is instantly upset and yells, "Twenty dollars! What do you think I am, some kind of whore?!"

The lawyer looks at her and says, "Well, we've already established that fact. Now we're just negotiating."

Good Scotch

A man walks into a bar in Ottawa and orders a glass of 12-year-old Scotch.

The bartender, believing that the customer will not be able to tell the difference, pours him a shot of the cheap three-year-old house Scotch that has been poured into an empty bottle of the good stuff.

The man takes a sip and spits the Scotch out on the bar and reams out the bartender. "This is the cheapest three-year-old Scotch you can buy. I'm not paying for it. Now, give me a good 12-year-old Scotch."

The bartender, now feeling a bit of a challenge, pours the guy a Scotch of much better quality—six-year-old Scotch. The man takes a sip and spits it out on the bar. "This is only six-year-old Scotch. I won't pay for this, and I insist on a good 12-year-old Scotch."

The bartender finally relents and serves the man his best quality 12-year-old Scotch. The man sips the drink and says, "Now that's more like it."

An old drunk from the end of the bar, who has witnessed the entire episode, walks over to the finicky Scotch drinker, sets a glass down in front of him and says, "What do you think of this?"

The Scotch expert takes a sip, and in disgust, violently spits out the liquid, yelling, "This tastes like piss!"

The old drunk replies, "That's right. Now guess how old I am."

How to Pick Up Women

Six Toronto bartenders are asked if they can figure out a woman's personality and how to approach her based on what she drinks. Though interviewed separately, the male bartenders concur on almost all counts. Here are the results:

Drink: Beer
Personality: Casual, low-maintenance, down to earth.

Your Approach: Challenge her to a game of pool.

Drink: Blender drinks
Personality: Flaky, annoying, a pain in the ass.

Your Approach: Avoid her, unless you want to be her cabin boy.

Drink: Mixed drinks
Personality: Older, has picky taste, knows what she wants.

Your Approach: You won't have to approach her. She'll send you a drink.

Drink: Wine (does not include white zinfandel; see below)
Personality: Conservative and classy, sophisticated.

Your Approach: Tell her you wish Reagan had had four more years. Alzheimer's and term limits be damned.

Drink: White zinfandel
Personality: Easy, thinks she is classy and sophisticated, actually has no clue.

Your approach: Make her feel smarter than she is.

Drink: Shots
Personality: Hangs out with frat-boys or wants to get drunk...and naked.

Your Approach: Easiest hit in the joint. Nothing to do but wait.

Beer

The biggest beer producers in the world meet for a conference, and at the end of the day, the presidents of all the beer companies decide to have a drink together at a bar.

The president of Budweiser naturally orders a Bud, the president of Miller orders a Miller, Adolph Coors orders a Coors, Geoff Molson orders a Molson and so on down the list.

The bartender asks Arthur Guinness what he wants to drink, and to everybody's amazement, he orders tea!

"Why don't you order a Guinness?" his colleagues ask suspiciously, wondering if they've stumbled on an embarrassing secret.

"Naaaah," replies Guinness. "If you guys aren't going to drink beer, then neither will I."

⫷ CHAPTER TWO ⫸
A Canadian in Nature

Big Canadian Animals

A Scotsman is invited for a visit to the home of his Canadian friend who lives in rural Saskatchewan.

Soon after the Scotsman arrives, he glances out the window to see a huge beast outside. He points and asks his Canadian friend, "Ach, lad, what's that?"

The Canadian replies, "Oh, that's a moose."

The Scotsman stares in disbelief and replies, "That's a moose?! Well, how big are yer cats then, laddie?"

Careful Wishing

Two men from Halifax are out fishing on a lake when they find a lamp floating in the water. One of the men picks it up and looks at the other man without much hope but decides to rub the lamp anyway.

A huge puff of smoke appears, and a genie pops out. Unfortunately, it is a low-level genie, and he can grant only one wish. The man who picked the lamp from the water requests that the entire lake be filled with Alexander Keith's ale.

Within seconds, the two men watch as mist forms on the water, and then all at once it turns a beautiful amber colour, and as that happens, the genie disappears.

The man with the lamp is ecstatic and looks at his buddy and soon realizes his friend is less than pleased.

He asks, "What's the matter, eh? What on earth could you be pissed about? Look at that...I even asked for Keith's, eh!"

The other man shakes his head and says, "Great thinking dere, Einstein. What are we supposed to do now—piss in the damn boat?"

Out Moose Hunting

Two guys from Labrador go moose hunting every year without success. Year after year, they hunt and hunt but always come home without a moose.

Finally, they come up with a foolproof plan. They rent an authentic cow moose costume and learn the mating call of a cow moose. Their plan is to hide inside the costume, lure in a bull moose, then come out of the costume, surprising the moose before shooting it.

So, they set themselves up on the edge of a clearing (in their costume) and give the moose love call. Before long, their call is answered by a large bull moose roaming around the edge of the forest. They call again, and the moose answers and moves a bit closer to them. They call again, and the moose answers, then comes crashing out of the forest and into the clearing.

As the moose's pounding hoof beats get closer to the men, the guy in front says, "Okay, let's get out and get him."

After a moment, the guy in the back shouts, "The zipper is stuck! What are we going to do?"

Q: What is the biggest lie told by an Alberta redneck cowboy?

A: I was just helping that sheep over the fence.

The guy in the front says, "Well, I'm going to start nibbling grass, but you'd better brace yourself!"

Strange Guide

A Native guy is guiding a group a British explorers across what are now the plains of Alberta. Suddenly he drops to his knees and puts his ear to the ground. The explorers stop and remain quiet while their guide listens to the rhythms of nature.

The Native guy says, "Buffalo come!"

The explorers are astonished at their guide's sensitivity to nature and ask, "How do you know that? How can you tell that the buffalo come?"

The Native guide lifts his ear off the ground and says, "Sticky!"

Strange Cock

A Manitoba farmer rears 25 young hens and one old cock. As the old cock can no longer handle his job efficiently, the farmer buys one young cock from the market and puts it in the pen with the old cock and the hens. The old cock greets the young cock.

Q: Where do polar bears vote?
A: The North Poll.

Old cock: "Welcome to the farm. We'll work together toward productivity."

Young cock: "Whattya mean? As far as I can tell, you're old and should be retired."

Old cock: "Young boy, there are 25 hens here. Can't I help you with some?"

Young cock: "No! Not even one. All of them will be mine."

Old cock: "In that case, I challenge you to a competition and, if I win, you will let me have one hen. If I lose, you can have them all."

Young cock: "Okay. What kind of competition?"

Old cock: "A 50-yard dash. From here to that tree. But because of my age, I hope you will allow me a head start for the first 10 yards?"

Young cock: "No problem! We'll race tomorrow morning."

The following morning, the young cock allows the old cock to have an early start to the race, and when the old cock crosses the 10-yard mark, the young cock chases him with all his might. He gets right behind the old cock in a matter of seconds and then he hears a loud bang. Before the young cock can overtake the old cock, he is shot dead by the farmer, who sighs and says, "Damn. That's the fifth gay chicken I bought this week."

Bear Hunting

Bob is excited about his new .308 shotgun and decides to try bear hunting.

He travels up to the Yukon, spots a small brown bear and shoots it. Soon after, there is a tap on his shoulder. He turns around to see a big black bear.

The black bear says, "That was a bad mistake. That bear was my cousin. I'm going to give you two choices. Either I maul you to death or we have sex." After briefly considering the choices, Bob decides to accept the latter alternative.

So the black bear has his way with Bob. Even though he is sore for two weeks, Bob soon recovers and vows to get revenge on the black bear. He heads out on another trip to the Yukon where he finds the black bear and shoots it dead. Right afterward, there is tap on his shoulder. He turns around and sees a huge grizzly bear.

The grizzly bear says, "That was a big mistake, Bob. That bear was my cousin, and you've got two choices: either I maul you to death or we have rough sex."

Again, Bob thinks it is better to cooperate with the grizzly bear than be mauled to death. So the grizzly has his way with Bob. Although he survives, it takes several months before Bob fully recovers.

Bob is completely outraged, so he heads back to the Yukon and manages to track down the grizzly bear and shoot it. He feels sweet revenge, but then, moments later, there is a tap on his shoulder.

> *Q:* What are the two seasons in Canada?
>
> *A:* Winter and July!

He turns around to find a giant polar bear standing there.

The polar bear looks at him and says, "Admit it, Bob, you don't come here for the hunting, do you?"

Walk in the Woods

A Baptist priest is walking in the mountains of British Columbia when he hears the ominous sounds of a bear behind him. "Oh Lord," prays the missionary, "grant in Thy goodness that the beast walking behind me is a good Christian bear."

> *Q:* What did the beaver say when his home was destroyed?
>
> *A:* Dam it!

And then, in the silence that follows, the missionary hears the bear praying too: "Oh Lord, I thank Thee for the food which I am about to receive."

Lumberjack

One day, while a big burly northern BC lumberjack is cutting a branch of a tree above a river, his axe falls into the water.

When he cries out, the Lord appears and asks, "Why are you crying?"

The lumberjack replies that his axe has fallen into the river, and he needs the axe to make his living.

The Lord goes down in the water and reappears with a golden axe. "Is this your axe?" the Lord says.

The lumberjack replies, "No."

The Lord again goes down and comes up with a silver axe. "Is this your axe?" the Lord asks.

Again, the lumberjack replies, "No."

The Lord goes down again and returns with an iron axe. "Is this your axe?" the Lord asks.

"Yes," the lumberjack replies.

The Lord is pleased with the man's honesty and gives him all three axes to keep, and the lumberjack goes home happy.

A few days later, the lumberjack is walking with his wife along the riverbank, and his wife slips and falls into the river.

When he cries out, the Lord again appears and asks him, "Why are you crying?"

"Oh Lord, my wife has fallen into the water!"

The Lord goes down into the water and comes up with Jennifer Lopez.

"Is this your wife?" the Lord asks.

"Yes," cries the lumberjack.

The Lord is furious. "You lied! That is an untruth!"

The lumberjack falls to his knees and cries, "Oh, forgive me, Lord. It's a misunderstanding. You see, if I had said 'no' to Jennifer Lopez, you would have come up with Catherine Zeta-Jones. Then if I also said 'no' to her, you would have come up with my wife. Had I then said 'yes,' you would have given me all three. Lord, I am a poor man and can't take care of three wives, and I love my wife such that I don't want her to have to share me with anyone, so that's why I said 'yes' to Jennifer Lopez."

The moral of the story: whenever a man lies, it is for a good and honourable reason, and for the benefit of others. Mostly his first lady!

Canadian, Eh?

A couple are at the airport in Phoenix awaiting their flight. They are dressed in heavy boots, parkas, scarves and gloves and are ready to head home to the Canadian winter.

An older American couple standing nearby is intrigued by their manner of dress. The wife says to her husband, "Look at that couple. I wonder where they're from?"

He replies, "How would I know?"

She counters, "You could go and ask them."

He says, "I don't really care. You want to know, so you go ask them."

The wife decides to do just that. She walks over to the couple and says, "Excuse me. I've been noticing the way you're dressed, and I was wondering...where are you from?"

The Canadian man replies, "Saskatoon, Saskatchewan."

The woman returns to her husband who asks, "So, where are they from?"

She replies, "I don't know. They don't speak English."

Fur Trapping

Q: What sort of ball doesn't bounce?
A: A snowball.

A young man gets a licence to trap furs in the Yukon for the winter. After buying the supplies he will need for his trip, he goes into a nearby saloon. Approaching the bartender he asks, "Is there any action to be had in this town?"

"What do ya mean by *action*?" the bartender replies.

"I mean, are there any women?" says the trapper.

"Nope, but there's always old Joe," says the bartender.

"No, thanks," says the trapper. "I don't go for that kind of stuff." And he leaves the saloon.

The next spring, the trapper returns to town. He has been snowed in for nine months and is in a slightly different frame of mind. He goes into the same bar and says, "Is there any action in town?"

"There's still old Joe," replies the same bartender.

"If I went for old Joe," the man says, "who would have to know about it?"

"Well," replies the bartender, "there's you, me, old Joe of course, and them three guys sitting at th'other end of the bar."

"Why do we need those three guys?" asks the trapper.

"To hold old Joe," replies the bartender. "He don't go for that kinda stuff, neither."

Gone Fishin'

After a day fishing on Lake Superior, a fisherman is walking from the pier carrying two brown trout in a bucket. A Conservation Officer approaches him and asks for his fishing licence.

The fisherman says to the officer, "I wasn't fishing, and I didn't catch these browns— they're my pets. Every day I come down to the water and dump these fish into the water and take them for a walk to the end of the pier and back. When I'm ready to go, I whistle, they jump back into the bucket and we go home. The officer, not believing the man, reminds him that it's illegal to fish without a licence.

Knock, knock.
Who's there?
Snow.
Snow who?
Snowbody but me.

The fisherman turns to the officer and says, "If you don't believe me, then watch this." He throws the trout back into the water.

The officer says, "Now whistle to your fish and show me that they will jump out of the water and into the bucket."

The fisherman says, "What fish?"

A Walk on the Beach

A ladies' man in Vancouver is walking on the beach one day when he spies a bottle lying in the sand. He picks it up, and when he wipes off the sand, a genie pops out and grants him one wish.

"I want to be rock hard and get plenty of ass for the rest of my life," says the man.

The genie smiles, and Poof! the guy turns into a toilet.

Up North

According to the Canadian Department of Fish and Wildlife, both male and female reindeer grow antlers in the summer each year. Male reindeer drop their antlers at the beginning of winter, usually late November to mid-December. Female reindeer retain their antlers until after they give birth in the spring.

Therefore, according to *every* historical rendition depicting Santa's reindeer, *every* one of them, from Rudolph to Blitzen, is a female.

We should've known that only women could drag a fat-ass man in a red velvet suit all around the world in one night and not get lost.

Warning!

In light of the rising frequency of human-grizzly bear conflicts, the Canadian Department of Fish and Wildlife is advising hikers, hunters and fishermen to take extra precautions and stay alert for bears while in the field.

"We advise that outdoorsmen wear noisy little bells on their clothing so as not to startle bears that aren't expecting them. We also advise outdoorsmen to carry pepper spray with them in case of an encounter with a bear. It's also a good idea to watch out for signs of recent bear activity. Outdoorsmen should recognize the difference between black bear and grizzly bear droppings. Black bear droppings are smaller and contain a lot of berries and squirrel fur. Grizzly bear droppings contain little bells and smell like pepper."

> *Q:* What is the scariest, most frightening and terrifying lake in Canada?
>
> *A:* Lake Erie.

Fishing Expert

On a cold winter day outside of Winnipeg, an old man walks out onto a frozen lake, cuts a hole in the ice, drops in his fishing line and waits for a fish to bite.

Q: How do Canadian environmental groups plan on using Hillary Clinton to stop the spread of Asian carp into the Great Lakes?

A: By having her go skinny dipping in Lake Michigan.

He is there for almost an hour without even a nibble when a young boy walks out onto the ice, cuts a hole in the ice not too far from the old man and drops in his fishing line.

It takes only a minute before a largemouth bass bites the boy's fishing hook, and the boy pulls in the fish.

The old man can't believe it but figures the boy was just lucky. But the boy drops in his line again and within just a few minutes pulls in another fish.

This goes on and on until finally the old man can't take it anymore since he hasn't caught a single fish during all this time. He walks up to the boy and says, "Son, I've been here for over an hour without even a nibble. You have been here only a few minutes and have caught about half a dozen fish! How do you do it?"

The boy says, "Roo raf roo reep ra rums rrarm!"

"What was that?" the old man asks.

Again the boy replies, "Roo raf roo reep ra rums rrram!"

"Look," says the old man, "I can't understand a word you're saying."

So the boy spits into his hand and says, "You have to keep the worms warm!"

Up North Trip

Mark and Steve go bear hunting out in the wilds of the Yukon. While Mark stays in the cabin, Steve goes out looking for a bear. He soon finds a huge bear and shoots at it but only wounds it. The enraged bear charges toward him, and Steve drops his rifle and starts running for the cabin as fast as he can.

He is running pretty fast, but the bear is just a little faster and gains on Steve with every step. Just as he reaches the open cabin door, he trips and falls down. Too close behind to stop, the bear trips over him and goes rolling into the cabin.

Steve jumps up, closes the cabin door and yells to Mark, "You skin this one while I go and get another one!"

The Other Side

Once upon a time, there was a river. The Fraser River, to be exact. On one side of the river lived the rabbit, and on the other side lived the bear.

One fine day, the bear is sitting on a stump, enjoying his breakfast of berries when he hears someone yelling at him. It's the rabbit.

"Hey! Hey, Teddy, get your butt over here. I have something to show you!"

"Not now! I'm eating."

"Oh, come on!" says the rabbit. "It's really important."

"No way."

"Please! It's urgent."

So the bear starts to swim across the wide river. It takes him all day and all night to get over to the other side. He nearly drowns. And when he finally gets there, he is panting and wheezing for air.

"Well, Rabbit," he pants. "What did you want to tell me?"

"Hey, Teddy," the rabbit says, "look how many berries are on the other side of the river."

Canadian Fisherman

An avid Hamilton fisherman decides to cross the Peace Bridge to Lewiston and fish the American side of the Niagara River.

Q: Why do birds fly south in the winter?

A: Because it's too far to walk.

He settles down on a quiet dock and begins to fill his bucket with some nice fish when an American game warden approaches him and says, "May I see your fishing licence, please?"

When the fisherman hands over his licence, the game warden laughs and says it's no good because it's a Canadian fishing licence.

At this point, the fisherman replies, "But I'm only catching Canadian fish."

The warden scratches his head for a moment and finally asks, "What do you mean?"

The fisherman reaches into his bucket and pulls out a fish and asks the warden, "What kind of fish is this?"

The warden looks at the fish and says, "It's a smallmouth bass."

The fisherman replies, "See what I mean? If it was an American fish, it would be a largemouth bass."

Fish Talk

Two fish are in a tank. One turns to the other and says, "Do you know how to drive one of these things?"

Texan Hunters

A group of Texans on their first hunting trip in Canada are camped on the shore of a lake in northern Manitoba.

They are greatly annoyed by the swarms of mosquitoes. They think that if they put out their campfire, the pests won't be able to find them, so they extinguish the flames. But then, in the pitch black, the Texans are able to make out the flashes of fireflies.

"It's no use!" one of the Texans says. "The varmints have their own flashlights."

Newfie Skier

A Newfie goes cross-country skiing. He is now crossing the Ontario–Manitoba border and intends to finish what he started.

Blondes on a Ranch

A blonde and a brunette are running a ranch together in Saskatchewan. They decide they need a bull to mate with their cows to increase their herd. The brunette takes their life savings of $600 and goes to Alberta to buy a bull.

She eventually meets with an old cowboy that will sell her a bull. "It's the only one I got for $599. Take it or leave it," says the old cowboy.

The brunette buys the bull and goes to the local telegraph office and says to the clerk, "I'd like to send a telegram to my friend in Saskatchewan that says, 'Have found the stud bull for our ranch. Bring the trailer.'"

Q: Why do so many Polish Canadians have names that end in "ski"?

A: Because they can't spell "toboggan."

The man behind the counter tells her, "Telegrams to anywhere in Canada are $.75 per word."

The brunette thinks about it for a moment, remembering she only has $1.00 left, and then makes a decision. "I'd like to send one word, please," she says.

"And what word would that be?" inquires the clerk.

"'Comfortable,'" replies the brunette.

The man says, "I'm sorry, Miss, but how is your friend gonna understand this telegram?"

The brunette replies, "My friend is blonde and reads real slow. So when she gets this, she will see 'com-for-da-bull.'"

⤜ CHAPTER THREE ⤛

A Canadian Plays Hockey—and Other Sports But Mostly Hockey

Lockout-a-Thon

Hundreds of professional hockey players in our own nation are locked out, living at well below the seven-figure salary level. And as if that isn't bad enough, they could be deprived of their life-giving pay for several months, possibly longer, as a result of the lockout situation.

But you can help! For only $20,835 a month—which is $694.50 per day (that's less than the cost of a large screen projection TV)—you can help an NHL player remain economically viable during his time of need. This contribution by no means solves the problem as it barely covers his annual minimum salary, but it's a start, and every little bit will help!

Although $700 a day may not seem like a lot of money to you, to an NHL player it could mean the difference between spending the lockout golfing in Florida or taking a Mediterranean cruise. For you, $700 is nothing more than a month's rent, part of your mortgage payment or half your annual vehicle licence renewal, but to a hockey player, $700 will partially replace his daily salary.

Your commitment of less than $700 a day will enable a hockey player to buy that home entertainment centre, trade in his year-old Lexus for a new Ferrari or enjoy a weekend in Vegas.

How will you know you're helping? Each month, you will receive a complete financial report on the player you sponsor. Detailed information about his stocks, bonds, RRSPs, real estate and other investment holdings will be mailed to your home. Plus, upon signing up for this program, you will receive an unsigned photo of the player lounging on a beach somewhere in the Caribbean during the lockout (for a signed photo, please include an additional $150). Put the photo on your refrigerator to remind you of other people's suffering.

To sponsor a locked-out NHL player, check one of the boxes below to indicate your preference:

☐ Forward   ☐ Defenceman   ☐ Goaltender

☐ Entire team (Please call our 900 number to ask for the cost of sponsoring a specific team; you will be billed $10 per minute.)

☐ Alexander Ovechkin (higher cost: $32,000 per day)

☐ Please charge my account $694.50 per day for the duration of the lockout.

☐ Please send me a picture of the player I have sponsored, along with my very own Donald Fehr (executive director of the NHLPA) pin to wear proudly on my hat (include $80 for hat).

Your Name: _____

Telephone: _____

☐ MasterCard   ☐ Visa

☐ American Express   ☐ Other

Credit Card #:_____ Exp. Date:_____

Good Seats

It's game seven of the Stanley Cup final, and a young man makes his way to his seat at centre ice. He sits down, noticing that the seat next to him is empty. He leans over and asks his neighbour if someone will be sitting there.

"No," says the older man. "The seat is empty."

"That's incredible," says the young man. "Who in their right mind would buy a seat like this for the Stanley Cup playoff and not use it?"

The older man says, "Well, actually, the seat belongs to me. I was supposed to come with my wife, but she passed away. This will be the first Stanley Cup that we haven't attended together since we got married in 1967."

"Oh, I'm sorry to hear that. That's terrible. But couldn't you find someone else, a friend or relative or even a neighbour to take the seat?"

The man shakes his head and says, "Nope. They're all at the funeral."

World's Shortest Book: *Don Cherry on Astrophysics*

News Alerts

The NHL Lockout is now in effect. Leafs fans are disappointed at the possibility of not being disappointed again this year.

The NHL lockout is serious business. We need the NHL. The NHL keeps white people occupied. Bored white people are dangerous.

At the Ball Game

Three older women are thrilled about seeing their first Blue Jays baseball game. They smuggle a bottle of Jack Daniels into the ballpark. The game is exciting, and the women are enjoying themselves immensely... mixing Jack Daniels with their pop. After a while, they realize that the bottle is almost empty and the game still has a lot of innings to go.

Q: What do the Montréal Canadiens have that the Toronto Maple Leafs don't?

A: Colour photographs of the Stanley Cup.

Based on the information given above, can you guess what inning it is and how many players are on base? Now think! Think some more! You're gonna love this. Answer: It's the bottom of the fifth, and the bags are loaded!

Adventure

One summer day on Vancouver Island, Mark and Tony decide to try bungee jumping.

Q: What is the hardest part about skating?

A: The ice.

After a full day of bungee fun, Mark says, "You know, Tony, we could make a lot of money running our own bungee jumping service in Mexico."

"You're right," replies Tony.

So Mark and Tony pool their money and buy everything they need to start their new venture:

Q: How do you know if you're a real hoser?

A: You own four pairs of skates but only one pair of shoes.

a tower, heavy-duty elastic cords and insurance, among other things.

They drive from Vancouver to Mexico and set up their equipment on the edge of a high cliff. While they construct the tower, a crowd assembles at the bottom of the cliff to watch.

Hours later, Mark and Tony finish building the tower and decide to test it out. Mark climbs the tower, straps himself in and jumps.

When he bounces back up, he has a few cuts and bruises. Tony tries to catch him, but Mark spirals back down. When Mark bounces up the next time, he's bruised and bleeding. Again, Tony reaches for his friend, and again, he misses.

When Mark comes back up a third time, he's brutally beaten, almost unconscious. Luckily, Tony catches him and drags him onto the platform.

"What happened?" Tony says, horrified. "Was the cord too long?"

Mark replies, "No, the cord is fine. But what the heck is a 'piñata'?"

Hockey Husband

A man is lying on the couch in his living room watching a hockey game. When his wife walks into the room a few minutes later, he says to her, "Just so you know, I never want to live in a vegetative state, dependent on some machine and fluids from a bottle. If that ever happens, just pull the plug."

His wife walks over to the TV, shuts it off and throws out all of his beer.

Olympic Newfie

A Russian and a Newfoundland wrestler are set to square off for the Olympic gold medal. Before the final match, the Newfie wrestler's trainer goes up to him and says, "Now, don't forget all the research we've done on this Russian. He's never lost a match because of this 'pretzel' hold he has. So whatever you do, do not let him get you in that hold! If he does, you're finished!"

The Newfie nods in acknowledgement. When the wrestling match begins, the Newfie and the Russian circle each other several times, looking for an opening.

All of a sudden, the Russian lunges forward, grabs the Newfie and wraps him up in the dreaded pretzel hold. A sigh of disappointment rises from the crowd, and the trainer buries his face in his hands, for he knows all is lost. He can't watch the inevitable happen.

Q: Why is the Hockey Hall of Fame in Toronto?

A: It's the only way the Stanley Cup will ever be in Toronto.

Suddenly, there is a blood-curdling scream, and the crowd cheers. The trainer raises his head just in time to see the Russian go flying up in the air. The Russian wrestler's back hits the mat with a thud, and the Newfoundlander collapses on top of him, making the pin and winning the match.

The Newfie trainer is astounded. When he finally gets his wrestler alone, he says, "How did you ever get out of that hold? No one has ever done it before!"

The wrestler replies, "Well, I was ready to give up when he got me in that hold, but at the last moment, I opened my eyes and saw a pair of testicles right in front of my face. I had nothing to lose, so with my last ounce of strength, I stretched out my neck and bit those babies just as hard as I could."

"Oh!" the trainer exclaims, "so that's what finished him off!"

"Not really," replies the Newfie wrestler. "You'd be amazed how strong you get when you bite your own nuts."

Back in the Day

Q: Why did the Canada goose run onto the soccer field?

A: Because the referee called a foul.

A young Vancouver man who is an avid golfer finds himself with a few hours to spare one afternoon. He figures if he hurries and plays fast, he can get in nine holes before he has to head home.

Just as he is about to tee off, an old gentleman shuffles onto the tee and asks if he can accompany the young man as he is golfing alone. Not wanting to be impolite, the young guy allows the old gent to join him.

To his surprise, the old man plays fairly quickly. He doesn't hit the ball far but plods along consistently and doesn't waste much time. Finally, they reach the ninth fairway, and the young man finds himself with a tough shot. There is a tall pine tree directly between his ball and the green.

After the young man takes several minutes thinking about how to hit the shot, the old man finally says, "You know, when I was your age, I hit the ball right over that tree."

With that challenge placed before him, the young man swings hard, hits the ball up, right smack into the top of the tree trunk and it thuds back on the ground not a foot from where it had originally lay.

The old man offers one more comment, "Of course, when I was your age, that pine tree was only three feet tall."

The Greatest One

A young hockey-loving kid dies and goes to heaven, where he meets St. Peter at the Pearly Gates.

"Do you want to join the Good Guys in heaven or the Bad Guys in heaven?" asks St. Peter.

"The Good Guys, of course," says the kid.

St. Peter starts to lead the boy through the crowd of people. Just then, one of the Good Guys appears, pushing everybody out of the way and stickhandling a puck through the crowd.

"If that bully is one of the Good Guys, what are the Bad Guys like?" asks the kid.

Q: What goes all around a hockey rink but never moves?

A: The boards.

"I know what you're thinking," replies St. Peter. "But that's not a Bad Guy. That's only God; sometimes he likes to pretend he's Wayne Gretzky."

Blonde Golf

Two young blonde Newfie women are playing golf at a foggy par three. They can see the flag but not the green. Each woman hits her ball anyway. When they walk over to the green, they discover one ball about three feet from the cup, while the other ball somehow has gone directly in.

The blondes try to figure out which ball belongs to whom, since they were both using Titlist number threes. Unable to decide, they return to the clubhouse and ask the golf pro for a ruling.

After hearing their story and congratulating them both on their superb shots under such adverse conditions, the pro asks, "Okay, so who was playing the yellow ball?"

Golf Therapy

While golfing with the Toronto Maple Leafs after another year of missing the playoffs, the team's physical therapist tees off, but she slices her shot and hits one of the players standing on the adjacent green. The player collapses in agony with his hand pressed firmly between his legs.

> **Q:** How can the Canadian men's Olympic ice hockey team hope to win?
>
> **A:** Play like the Canadian women.

The physical therapist runs over to him and says, "Don't worry. I have medical training. I can help reduce the pain."

The player agrees to let her see what she can do. So she unzips his pants and begins to massage his privates.

After a minute or two of vigorous rubbing, she asks, "Does that feel better?"

"Mmmmm, yes," the player replies. "Thank you. But it was my thumb you broke."

Sports and Society

A recent study by the Canadian National Sports Society examined the recreational preferences of Canadians from all social and economic levels. Below are the most interesting findings from the study:

1. The sport of choice for the unemployed or the incarcerated is basketball.

2. The sport of maintenance staff and grounds-keepers is football.

3. The sport of the frontline service worker is bowling.

4. The sport of the supervisor is baseball.

5. The sport for the middle-management type is tennis.

6. The sport for the upwardly mobile corporate bigwig is golf.

The conclusion of the report: the higher you are on the corporate ladder, the smaller your balls.

Newfie at a Ball Game

On a visit to Toronto, a Newfie is attending his first baseball game. After a base hit, he hears the fans roar, "Run, run!" So when the next batter makes a good hit, the Newfie joins in the shouts of "Run, run!"

Wanting to show how quickly he has picked up the rules of the game, the Newfie stands up when the third batter slams a hit, and the Newfie leads the chorus of "Run, run!"

The next batter holds his swing at three and two, and as the umpire calls a walk, the Newfie stands up again and yells, "Run, run!" As everybody around him starts to laugh, the Newfie sits down all red in the face and totally confused as to what he has done wrong.

Q: What is the favourite chant before the start of a curling match?

A: Are you ready to rock?!

The man in the seat next to the Newfie leans over and says, "He doesn't have to run; he's got four balls."

The Newfie immediately stands up and shouts, "Walk with pride, man! Walk with pride!"

National Pride

Two American men board an American Airlines flight out of Salt Lake City after the Olympic gold medal hockey game. One man sits in the window seat and the other sits in the middle seat. Just before take-off, a Canadian boards the plane and takes the aisle seat. After take-off, the Canadian kicks his shoes off, wiggles his toes and is settling in when the American in the window seat says, "I think I'll get up and get a beer."

> News Bulletin reported in St. John's, Newfoundland: "A terrible tragedy has occurred down at the local curling club. They all drowned during spring training."

"No problem," says the Canadian, "I'll get it for you."

While the Canadian guy is gone, one of the Americans picks up the Canadian's shoe and spits in it. When the Canadian returns with the beer, the other American says, "That looks good; I think I'll have one too." Again, the Canadian obligingly goes to fetch a beer, and while he is gone, the other American picks up the other shoe and spits in it. When the Canadian returns to his seat, they all sit back and enjoy the rest of the flight. As the plane is landing, the Canadian slips his feet into his shoes and knows immediately what has happened.

"Why does it have to be this way?" the Canadian says. "How long must this go on? This fighting between our nations, this hatred, this animosity? This spitting in shoes and pissing in beers?"

A Russian Commenting on Baseball

In Winnipeg in 1995, Russian hockey player Alexei Zhamnov saw his first minor league baseball game and was completely underwhelmed. Midway through the game, he incredulously asked, "Do they shower after this?"

Trust Issues

A huge fire erupts at the arena of an All-Star hockey game. Three fans wearing the jerseys of their favourite teams are stranded on the roof: a Montréal fan, a Boston fan and a Detroit fan. The fire department arrives with a blanket and yells to the Canadiens fan to jump. He jumps, and the firefighters quickly move the blanket to the right, and the Canadiens fan hits the sidewalk with a splat.

Q: What do hockey players and magicians have in common?

A: They both do hat tricks.

The firefighters yell to the Boston fan to jump. He says he won't jump. The firefighters explain that they hate the Canadiens. The fan says he hates them too and decides to jump. Again, the firefighters move the blanket to the right, and the fan hits the ground with a splat.

Finally, they call to the Detroit Red Wings fan to jump. He says he won't jump. The firefighters say they really hate the Bruins, to which the man replies, "I don't trust you. Lay the blanket down, and then I'll jump!"

Ski Accident

A husband and wife are on a ski hill in Whistler, BC. The wife complains to her husband that she is in dire need of a restroom. He tells her not to worry and that he is sure there is relief waiting at the top of the lift in the form of a restroom for skiers in distress. He is wrong, of course, and the wife's pain does not go away.

Q: Why are the Toronto Maple Leafs like Canada Post?

A: They both wear uniforms and neither delivers.

The husband, picking up on the intensity of his wife's discomfort, suggests that since she is wearing an all-white ski outfit, she should go off in the woods to relieve herself. No one will even notice, he assures her. The white snow will provide more than adequate camouflage. So she heads for the tree line, begins disrobing and proceeds to do her thing.

If you've ever parked on the side of a slope, then you know there is a right way and a wrong way to set up your skis so you don't move. Yup, you guessed it. The woman positioned her skis the wrong way.

Without warning, the woman finds herself skiing backwards, out of control, racing through the trees, somehow missing all of them and heading into another slope. Her derriere is still bare, her ski pants are down around her knees and she is picking up speed all the while.

She continues on backwards, totally out of control, creating an unusual vista for other skiers. The woman skies—if you define that verb loosely—back under the lift and finally collides violently with a pylon. The bad news is that she breaks her arm and is unable to pull up her ski pants. At long last, her husband arrives, pulls up her pants and summons the ski patrol, who transport her to a hospital.

In the emergency room, the woman is regrouping when a man with an obviously broken leg is put in the bed next to hers.

"So. How did you break your leg?" she asks, making small talk.

"It was the darndest thing you ever saw," he replies. "I was riding up a ski lift, and suddenly I couldn't believe my eyes. Some crazy woman was skiing backwards down the mountain with her bare bottom hanging out and her pants down around her knees. I leaned over to get a better look, and I guess I didn't realize how far I'd moved. I fell out of the lift. How did you break your arm?"

What Ya Got?

Bill: "Hey Phil, are you going fishing?"

Phil: "Yup!"

Bill: "You got worms?"

Phil: "Yup, but I'm still going!"

Golf Lessons from the Past

One sunny day in Kelowna, Jim and Bob are out golfing. Jim slices his ball deep into a wooded ravine. He grabs his eight-iron and proceeds down the embankment into the ravine in search of his ball.

The brush is quite thick, but Jim searches diligently and suddenly spots something shiny. As he gets closer, he realizes that the shiny object is in fact an eight-iron in the hands of a skeleton lying near an old golf ball.

Jim calls out to his golfing partner in an agitated voice, "Hey, Bob, come here! I got trouble down here!"

Bob runs over to the edge of the ravine and calls out, "What's the matter, Jim?"

Jim shouts back, "Throw me my seven-iron! You can't get out of here with an eight-iron!"

A Blue Jay in Court

One of the Toronto Blue Jays' best players is called as character witness in a matrimonial case. When he is asked about his profession, he replies, "I am the greatest baseball player in the world!"

After the case is over, the player is teased by his teammates. "How could you stand up in court and say a thing like that?" one of them asks.

"Well," the ballplayer replies, "you must remember—I was under oath."

Beethoven's Ninth Symphony

The Vancouver Symphony Orchestra is rehearsing Beethoven's "Ninth Symphony." There is an extensive section where the bass players don't play for about 20 minutes. One of the bass players suggests that, rather than stand around on stage looking bored and stupid, they should all just file offstage during the next performance and then return when they need to play.

On the night of the performance, the bass players file offstage as planned. The last player has barely left the stage when the leader suggests, "Hey, we've got 20 minutes. Let's run across the street to the bar for a few!"

The idea is met with great approval. So off they go, tuxedos and all, to loosen up at the nearest bar. Fifteen minutes and a few rounds later, one of the bass players says, "Shouldn't we be heading back? It's almost time for us to play."

The leader announces, "Oh, don't worry. We have some extra time—I played a little joke on the conductor. Before the performance started, I tied string around each page of his score so that he has to untie each page to turn it. The performance will drag on for a bit. We have time for another round!"

So after another round of drinks, sloshed and staggering, the bass players finally make their way across the street to finish Ludwig's Ninth.

Upon appearing on the stage, they immediately notice the conductor's haggard, drawn and livid expression.

"Gee," one of the bass players says, "why do you suppose he looks so tense?"

"You'd be tense, too," says the leader with a laugh. "It's the bottom of the ninth, the score is tied and the basses are loaded."

Trouble in Hell

One day, Satan is out for a walk through Hell, making sure things are running smoothly. When he gets to the Lake of Fire, he sees a man sitting by the lake, relaxing in a lawn chair and not sweating or looking uncomfortable at all.

Q: Did you hear about the change Canada Post made to their stamps?

A: There used to be Leafs players on them, but people didn't know which side to spit on!

Perplexed, Satan approaches the man and asks, "Young man, are you not hot or bothered by this heat?"

The man replies, "Oh no, not at all. I lived in downtown Ottawa, and this weather is just like a typical July day in the city."

Satan thinks that this is not a good sign, so he rushes back to his office and turns up the heat in Hell another 100 degrees. Satisfied with himself,

Satan again returns to the Lake of Fire to check on the young man.

When Satan gets there, the man is showing a few beads of sweat on his forehead but that is all.

Again, Satan asks the Ottawa native, "Are you hot and uncomfortable yet?"

The young man looks up and says, "No, the temperature is just like a hot August day in Ottawa. I'm coping with it just fine."

Satan decides he has to do something drastic to make this man's stay in Hell unpleasant. He goes back to his office, turns the heat all the way down and then turns up the air conditioning.

The temperature in Hell quickly drops well below zero. As he approaches the Lake of Fire, Satan notices that it is now frozen over. He also sees the young man jumping up and down wildly, waving his arms and yelling into the air.

"This looks promising!" thinks Satan. Going closer, he finally hears what the man is shouting: "The Leafs have won the Stanley Cup! The Leafs have won the Stanley Cup!"

⋘ CHAPTER FOUR ⋙
A Canadian Goes to Church

Lord's Army

A man is leaving a church in Victoria on Christmas Day, and the old preacher is standing at the door as he always is, ready to shake the hands of his parishioners as they leave. He grabs the man's arm and pulls him aside.

The pastor says to him, "You need to join the Army of the Lord!"

"I'm already in the Army of the Lord, Pastor," replies the man.

The old preacher says, "Is that so? Then how come I don't see you in church except at Christmas and Easter?"

The man whispers back, "I'm in the secret service."

Sober Up

A man sobering up from a night of partying on the streets of Toronto is sitting through the Sunday sermon, finding it long and boring. Still feeling hungover and tired, he finally nods off.

The priest, who has been watching him all along and noticing his apparent hangover, is disgusted.

At the end of the sermon, the preacher decides to make an example of the man.

He says to his congregation, "All those wishing to have a place in heaven, please stand."

Everyone in the church stands up except, of course, the sleeping man.

Then the preacher says even more loudly, "And he who would like to find a place in hell please stand up!"

The hungover man has just caught the last part of what the preacher says and groggily stands up. He suddenly notices that he's the only person standing.

Confused and embarrassed, he says, "I don't know what we're voting on here, Father, but it sure seems like you and me are the only ones standing for it!"

Drinking Buddy

Arthur is sitting on the patio outside his local pub one summer day in St. John's, Newfoundland, enjoying a pint of beer and generally feeling good about himself and the world. Suddenly, a nun appears at his table and starts decrying the evils of drink.

Q: When in heaven, how can you tell which people are the Newfies?

A: They are the ones who want to go back home.

"You should be ashamed of yourself, young man! Drinking is a sin! Alcohol is the blood of the devil!" cries the nun.

Now, Arthur is pretty annoyed about the nun's outburst and goes on the offensive.

"How do you know, Sister?"

"My Mother Superior told me so."

"But have you ever had a drink yourself? How can you be sure that what you're saying is true?"

"Don't be ridiculous—of course I have never taken alcohol myself!"

"Then let me buy you a drink. If you still believe afterward that alcohol is evil, I will give up drink for life."

"How could I, a nun, sit outside this public house drinking?!"

"I'll get the barman to put your drink in a teacup for you; no one will know."

The nun reluctantly agrees, so Arthur goes inside the bar.

"Another pint for me, and a triple vodka on the rocks," he tells the bartender. He then lowers his voice and says, "And could you put the vodka in a teacup?"

"Oh, no! It's not that drunken nun again, is it?"

Church Bloopers

The following are actual church bulletin bloopers found in churches across Canada.

- Scouts are saving aluminum cans, bottles and other items to be recycled. Proceeds will be used to cripple children.

- The Outreach Committee has enlisted 25 visitors to make calls on people who are not afflicted with any church.

- Evening massage: 6:00 PM.

- The pastor would appreciate it if the ladies of the congregation would lend him their electric girdles for the pancake breakfast next Sunday morning.

- The audience is asked to remain seated until the end of the recession.

- The Low Self-esteem Support Group will meet on Thursday at 7:00 PM. Please use the back door.

- Ushers will eat latecomers.

- The third verse of "Blessed Assurance" will be sung without musical accomplishment.

- For those of you who have children and don't know it, we have a nursery downstairs.

- The Reverend Merriwether spoke briefly, much to the delight of the audience.

- The pastor will preach his farewell message, after which the choir will sing "Break Forth into Joy."

- Next Sunday, Mrs. Vinson will be soloist for the morning service. The pastor will then speak on "It's a Terrible Experience."

- As a result of the Rector's illness, Wednesday's healing services will be discontinued until further notice.

- Stewardship Offertory: "Jesus Paid It All."

- The music for today's service was all composed by George Friedrich Handel in celebration of the 300th anniversary of his birth.

- Remember in your prayers the many who are sick of our church and community.

- The eighth-graders will be presenting Shakespeare's Hamlet in the church basement on Friday at 7:00 PM. The congregation is invited to attend this tragedy.

- The concert held in Fellowship Hall was a great success. Special thanks is sent to the minister's daughter, who laboured the whole evening at the piano, which as usual fell upon her.

- A song fest was hell at the Methodist church Wednesday.

- Today's Sermon: "How Much Can a Man Drink?" with hymns from a full choir.

- Hymn 43: "Great God, What Do I See Here?" Preacher: The Reverent Horace Blodgett.

- Hymn 47: "Hark! An Awful Voice Is Sounding."

- In a church bulletin during the minister's illness: God is good. Dr. Hargreaves is better.

- Potluck supper: Prayer and medication to follow.

- Don't let worry kill you off—let the church help.

- The 1997 Spring Council Retreat will be hell on May 10 and 11.

- Pastor is on vacation. Massages can be given to church secretary.

Broken Down

A priest and a nun are travelling to Winnipeg late at night when their car breaks down in a small town. They can't get it fixed, so they decide to spend the night in a hotel. The only hotel in the town has just one room available. The priest and nun discuss how they should handle the sleeping arrangements.

Priest: "Sister, I don't think the Lord would have a problem, under the circumstances, if we spent the night together in this one room. I'll sleep on the couch, and you can have the bed."

Nun: "I think that would be okay."

They prepare for bed, and each one takes their agreed sleeping spot in the room.

Ten minutes later...

Nun: "Father, I'm terribly cold."

Priest: "Okay, I'll get you a blanket."

Ten minutes later...

Nun: "Father, I'm still terribly cold."

Priest: "Okay, I'll get you another blanket."

Ten minutes later...

Nun: "Father, I'm still terribly cold. I don't think the Lord would mind if we acted as man and wife just for this one night."

Priest: "You're probably right—get up and get your own blanket!"

Proof that Jesus was Québecois

1. He never got married.
2. His last request was a drink.
3. He didn't speak English.

Finding God

A Regina couple has two little mischievous boys, ages 8 and 10. Their sons are always getting into trouble, and the parents know that if any mischief occurs in their town, their sons usually get the blame.

The boys' mother hears that a new clergyman in town has been successful in disciplining children, so she asks him if he could speak with her sons. The clergyman agrees and asks to see the boys individually.

The mother sends her eight-year-old to see the clergyman first thing in the morning, with the older boy to see the clergyman in the afternoon.

The clergyman, a huge man with a booming voice, sits the young boy down and asks him sternly, "Where is God?"

The boy's mouth drops open, but he makes no response and just sits there silently.

The clergyman repeats the question more loudly. "Where is God?!"

Again, the boy makes no attempt to answer.

The clergyman raises his voice even more and shakes his finger in the boy's face and bellows, "Where is God?!"

The boy screams and bolts from the room. He runs directly home and dives into his closet, slamming the door behind him.

When his older brother finds him in the closet a few minutes later, he asks, "What happened?"

The younger brother, gasping for breath, replies, "We are in real *big* trouble this time! God is missing, and they think we did it!"

Physically Fitter

As Bill is approaching mid-life, physically he is a mess. Not only is he still single and going bald, but working in downtown Toronto for 25 years has also given him a large pot belly. Sitting on the GO Train for 45 minutes to work, then sitting all day at his computer and through long meetings and then 45 minutes back on the train home has really taken a lot out of him. The last straw comes when he asks a female co-worker out on a date, and she all but laughs in his face.

"That does it," he says to himself. "I'm going to start a whole new regimen."

Bill starts attending aerobics classes and works out with weights. He also changes his diet and gets an expensive hair transplant. In six months, he has transformed himself. Again, he asks the same female co-worker out on a date, and this time she accepts.

On the night of the date, Bill is all dressed up, looking better than he ever has. He stands poised to ring the woman's doorbell when a bolt of lightning strikes him and knocks him off his feet. As he lies there on the doorstep dying, he turns his eyes toward the heavens and says, "Why, God? Why now? After all I've been through, how could you do this to me?"

From above comes a voice, "Sorry. I didn't recognize you."

On a Mission

A Canadian missionary is sent into the deepest darkest depths of Africa to live with a local tribe. He spends years with the people, teaching them to read, write and practice good Christian values. One thing he particularly stresses is the evil of sexual sin—thou must not commit adultery or fornication!

One day the wife of one of the tribesmen gives birth to a white baby. The village is shocked, and the people send the chief to talk with the missionary.

"You have taught us of the evils of sexual sin, yet here a black woman gives birth to a white child. You are the only white man who has ever set foot in our village. Anyone can see what's going on here," says the chief.

The missionary replies, "No, no, my good man. You are mistaken. What you have here is a natural occurrence—what is called an albino. Look to thy yonder field. See the field of white sheep, and yet among them is one black one. Nature does this on occasion."

The chief pauses for a moment, then says, "Tell you what...you don't say anything about the sheep, and I won't say anything about the white baby."

Helping Hand

One summer afternoon, a young boy named Alan is playing outdoors on his family's farm in rural Saskatchewan. He uses his mother's broom as a horse and has a wonderful time until it starts to get dark outside.

Alan leaves the broom on the back porch and goes inside the house. His mother is cleaning up the kitchen when she realizes that her broom is missing. She asks her son about the broom, and he tells her it's on the back porch.

She then asks him to please go get it. Alan informs his mom that he's afraid of the dark and doesn't want to go outside to get the broom.

His mother smiles and says, 'The Lord is out there too; don't be afraid."

Alan opens the back door just a crack and says, "Lord, if you're out there, hand me the broom!"

Me Too!

I once saw this guy on a bridge in Windsor, Ontario, about to jump. I ran over to him and said, "Don't do it!"

The distraught man said, "Nobody loves me."

I said, "God loves you. Do you believe in God?"

He said, "Yes."

I said, "Are you a Christian or a Jew?"

He said, "A Christian."

I said, "Me, too! Protestant or Catholic?"

He said, "Protestant."

I said, "Me, too! What franchise?"

He said, "Baptist."

I said, "Me, too! Northern Baptist or Southern Baptist?"

He said, "Northern Baptist."

I said, "Me, too! Northern Conservative Baptist or Northern Liberal Baptist?"

He said, "Northern Conservative Baptist."

I said, "Me, too! Northern Conservative Baptist Great Lakes Region, or Northern Conservative Baptist Eastern Region?"

He said, "Northern Conservative Baptist Great Lakes Region."

I said, "Me, too! Northern Conservative Baptist Great Lakes Region Council of 1879, or Northern Conservative Baptist Great Lakes Region Council of 1912?"

He said, "Northern Conservative Baptist Great Lakes Region Council of 1912."

I said, "Die, heretic!" And I pushed him over.

Ole Canada

About 150 years ago in Montréal, the women of high society had to go through quite the gymnastics to squeeze themselves into what fashion deemed beautiful.

One of the most popular torture devices of the time was a kirtle, a garment made to fit exceedingly tight over the buttocks, in order to give the effect of greater prominence. To hide the excess strain on the flesh underneath, the ladies wore several overskirts.

A story was once told about how a certain, shall we say, ample, noble Catholic dame found herself late for church on Easter morning and was in such a hurry that she forgot to secure her kirtle tightly. As she neared the Notre-Dame Cathedral, she met a small boy whose eyes suddenly widened upon seeing her

"Tell me, little man," she says, "is Mass out yet?"

"No," replies the boy, "but it will be soon if you take anymore steps!"

At the Ball Game

Sitting behind a couple of nuns at a Blue Jays baseball game, three men decide to badger the nuns in an effort to get them to move because their habits are partially blocking their view of the game.

In a loud voice, the first guy says, "I think I'm going to move to Montréal! There are only 100 nuns living there."

The second guy speaks up and says, "I want to go to Calgary! There are only 50 nuns living there."

The third guy says, "I want to go to Vancouver! There are only 25 nuns living there."

One of the nuns turns around, looks at the men, and in a very sweet, calm voice says, "Why don't you go to hell. There aren't any nuns there."

Conversion

John Smith is the only English Protestant to move into a large French Catholic neighbourhood in the east end of Montréal. On the first Friday of Lent, John is outside grilling a big juicy steak on his grill. Meanwhile, all of his neighbours are eating cold tuna for supper.

This routine takes place on each Friday of Lent. On the last Friday of Lent, three of the neighbourhood men get together and decide that something has to be done about John because he is tempting them to eat meat each Friday of Lent, and they can't take it anymore.

The men decide to try to convert John to Catholicism. They go talk to him and are overjoyed when John agrees to join all of his neighbours and become a Catholic. They take him to church, and the priest sprinkles holy water over him and says, "You were born a Baptist, you were raised a Baptist and now you are a Catholic."

The men are so relieved that their biggest Lenten temptation is resolved. The next year's Lenten season rolls around. The first Friday of Lent arrives, and at supper time, when the men of the neighbourhood are setting down to their tuna dinner, comes the wafting smell of beef cooking on a grill. The men in the neighbourhood can't believe their noses! What is going on they wonder.

They call each other up and decide to meet over in John's yard to see if he had forgotten it is the first Friday of Lent.

The group arrive just in time to see John standing over his grill with a small pitcher of water. He is sprinkling water over his steak on the grill, saying, "You were born a cow, you were raised a cow and now you are a fish."

Gates of Heaven

A woman from Toronto arrives at the Gates of Heaven. While she is waiting for St. Peter to greet her, she peeks through the gates.

She sees a beautiful banquet table filled with all kinds of food and drink. Sitting around the table are her parents and all the other people she has loved and who have died before her. They see her and begin calling to her: "Hello! Good to see you. How are you? We've been waiting for you!"

When St. Peter returns to the Gates of Heaven, the woman says to him, "This is such a wonderful place! How do I get in?"

"You have to spell a word," St. Peter tells her.

"Which word?" the woman asks.

"Love."

The woman correctly spells "love," and St. Peter welcomes her into Heaven.

About a year later, St. Peter goes to the woman and asks her to watch the Gates of Heaven for him that day.

While the woman is guarding the Gates of Heaven, her husband arrives.

"I'm surprised to see you," the woman says. "How have you been?"

"Oh, I've been doing pretty well since you died," her husband tells her. "I married the beautiful young nurse who took care of you while you were ill. And then I won Lotto Max. I sold the little house you and I lived in and bought a huge mansion. My wife and I travelled all around the world. We were on vacation in Cancun, and I went water skiing today. I fell and hit my head, and here I am. What a bummer. How do I get in?"

"You have to spell a word," the woman tells him.

"Which word?" her husband asks.

"Saskatchewan."

Save Me, Lord

There is a flood in a small Manitoba town.

One man says to everyone, "I'll stay with my house! God will save me!"

The flood rises higher, and a boat comes and the man in it says, "Come on, mate, get in!"

"No," replies the man. "God will save me!"

The flood gets very high now, and the man has to stand on the roof of his house.

A helicopter soon arrives and offers to rescue the man.

"No, thanks," says the man. "God will save me!"

Eventually, the man drowns.

He gets to the Gates of Heaven and says to God, "Why didn't you save me?"

God replies, "For goodness sake! I sent a boat and a helicopter. What more do you want!"

Jesus' Name

A group of biblical scholars from Montréal are involved in a heated discussion about how Jesus of Nazareth was named. How did he become known as the Messiah or Christ?

One of the scholars argues that the name was a Greek corruption of Aramaic, and purists and fundamentalists ought to use the name Joshua. Another argued that Joshua was Hebrew, not Aramaic, to which a third argued that Hebrew should be used because Jesus was said to be the King of the Jews.

The debate raged on and on and became more and more sophisticated and confusing. Finally, an old professor known for his wisdom intervenes. He informs the group that he knows how Jesus was named. "When Jesus was born, a star shone in the sky, and three wise men from the East travelled to Bethlehem. They had travelled for days, suffered great deprivation, and when they finally got to Bethlehem, they got lost trying to find the manger. Finally, after much ado, and in rather foul moods, they reached the manger and entered the stall. As one of them came through the door, he tripped on the threshold and fell into the wall hitting his head. 'Jesus Christ!' he screamed, and that is how the baby was named."

Out of the Convent

Two old Scottish nuns have just arrived in Canada. One says to the other, "I hear that the people of this country actually eat dogs."

"That's odd," her companion replies, "but if we shall live in Canada, we might as well do as the Canadians do."

Nodding emphatically, the Mother Superior points to a hotdog vendor, and the nuns both walk toward him. "Two dogs, please," says the Mother Superior.

The vendor is only too pleased to oblige. He wraps the hot dogs in foil and hands them over the counter. Excited, the nuns quickly unwrap their dogs.

The Mother Superior is first to open hers. She begins to blush and, then, staring at it for a moment, leans over to the other nun and whispers cautiously, "What part did you get?"

Sisters

A man is driving down a deserted stretch of highway in rural Nova Scotia when he notices a sign out of the corner of his eye. It reads:

Sisters of St. Francis
House of Prostitution
10 kilometres

He thinks the sign is just a figment of his imagination and drives on without giving it a second thought. Soon he sees another sign that says:

Sisters of St. Francis
House of Prostitution
5 kilometres

Suddenly, he begins to realize that these signs are for real. He continues driving and sees a third sign:

Sisters of St. Francis
House of Prostitution
Next Right

The man's curiosity gets the best of him and he pulls into the drive. On the far side of the parking lot is a sombre-looking stone building with a small sign next to the door that simply says

Sisters of St. Francis.

He climbs the steps and rings the bell. The door is answered by a nun in a long black habit who asks, "What may we do for you, my son?"

The man replies, "I saw your signs along the highway and was interested in possibly doing business."

"Very well, my son. Please follow me."

He is led through many winding passages and is soon quite disoriented. The nun stops at a closed door and tells the man, "Please knock on this door."

He does as he is told, and the door is answered by another nun in long habit who is holding a tin cup. This nun says, "Please place $50 in the cup, then go through the large wooden door at the end of this hallway."

He gets $50 out of his wallet and places it in the cup. He trots eagerly down the hall and slips through the door, pulling it shut behind him. As the door locks behind him, he finds himself back in the parking lot, facing another small sign:

Go in peace.
You have just been screwed
by the Sisters of St. Francis.

Into Hell

Montréal nun Sister Margaret dies, and through some error finds herself in hell.

She immediately calls Saint Peter and says, "This is Sister Margaret. There's been a terrible mistake!"

She explains the situation, and Saint Peter says he'll get right on it. The next day, the nun doesn't hear from Saint Peter, so she calls him again. "Please set this error straight before tomorrow," she begs. "There's an orgy planned for tonight, and everyone *must* attend!"

"Of course, Sister," he says. "I'll get you out of there right away."

Apparently, her plight slips his mind yet again, and the following morning Saint Peter receives another phone call from hell. He picks up the receiver with trepidation in his heart and listens.

He hears the following, "Hey, Pete, this is Maggie. Never mind!"

CHAPTER FIVE

A Canadian in Lust

All Hands

Every time Larry walks into his Newfie room-mate's room, he catches Barry masturbating. Larry finally realizes that this is a serious problem, so he sets Barry up with a beautiful woman.

One day, Larry walks into his apartment, and there is his friend Barry masturbating furiously.

Larry says, "Barry, what are you doing? I fixed you up with a beautiful woman!"

Barry replies, "Her arm got tired."

Canadian in a Park

Jennifer is in a park in Vancouver, attempting to strike up a conversation with the attractive gentle-man reading a book on a blanket beside her.

"Hello, sir," she says. "Do you like movies?"

"Yes, I do," he responds, returning immediately to his book.

Jennifer tries another route, saying, "Do you enjoy going to the movies?"

"Yes, I do," he responds before returning to his book.

Undaunted, Jennifer asks, "Do you like pussy-cats?"

Q: Why did the Conservative politician close his eyes during sex?

A: Because he doesn't like to see a woman enjoy herself.

With that, the man drops his book and pounces on Jennifer, making love to her in the park.

As the cloud of lust begins to settle, Jennifer drags herself into a sitting position and pants, "How did you know that was what I wanted?"

The man thinks for a second then says, "How did you know my name was Katz?"

Innocence Lost

A Montréaler and his Newfie girlfriend are necking in his car, when he suddenly stops and says, "You wanna get in the backseat?"

His girlfriend replies, "No way! I want to stay up front with you."

Country Encounter

One day, farmer Jones is in Regina to pick up supplies for his farm. He walks to the hardware store and buys a bucket and an anvil, then he stops by the livestock dealer to buy a couple of chickens and a goose.

Now he has a problem: how to carry all of his purchases home?

The livestock dealer says, "Why don't you put the anvil in the bucket, carry the bucket in one hand, put a chicken under each arm and carry the goose in your other hand."

"Hey, thanks!" the farmer says and walks away.

While walking down the street, he meets a fair young lady with rather large beautiful breasts. She tells him that she is lost and asks, "Can you tell me how to get to 1515 Mockingbird Lane?"

The farmer says, "Well, as a matter of fact, I'm going to visit my brother at 1540 Mockingbird Lane. Come with me. We'll take a short cut and go down this alley. We'll save half the time to get there."

The young woman says, "How do I know that when we get into the alley you won't hold me up against the wall, pull up my dress and ravish me?"

Q: Why is Mitt Romney considering moving to Canada?

A: Because his penis size will increase from 6 inches to 15.24 centimetres!

The farmer replies, "I'm carrying a bucket, an anvil, two chickens and a goose. How in the world could I possibly hold you up against the wall and do that?"

"Easy, silly!" says the woman. "Set the goose down, put the bucket over the goose, put the anvil on top of the bucket and I'll hold the friggen chickens!"

How to Impress a Canadian Woman

- Compliment her.
- Cuddle her.
- Kiss her.
- Tease her.
- Comfort her.
- Protect her.
- Hug her.
- Wine and dine her.
- Buy things for her.
- Listen to her.
- Care for her.
- Stand by her.
- Love her.
- Go to the ends of the earth for her.

How to Impress a Canadian Man

- Show up naked.
- Bring beer.

Confusion

Police in St. John's, Newfoundland, arrest a 30-year-old shop assistant after he is found lying naked with a mannequin in a store window.

"We found several bite marks on other manne-quins as well," a police officer tells the CBC News. "The suspect said he got somewhat confused after purchasing a book called *Making Love for Dummies*."

Daughters

An Englishman, a Scot and a Newfie are having a conversation about their daughters.

The Englishman says, "I found a packet of ciga-rettes in my daughter's bedroom. I didn't even know she smokes."

The Scottish man says, "Well, that's nothing. I found a bottle of whiskey in my daughter's bed-room. I didn't even know she drinks."

Then finally the Newfie says, "Ha! Consider yourselves lucky! The other day I found a packet of condoms in my daughter's bedroom. I didn't even know she has a dick!"

Late Night

A man is walking home late at night in the red light district of Montréal when he sees a woman in the shadows.

"Twenty bucks," she says to the man as he passes by.

The man has never been with a hooker before, so he thinks to himself, "What the hell; it's only $20."

They're going at it for a minute when all of a sud-den a light flashes on them. It's a police officer.

Q: How do you know Adam was a Canadian?

A: Who else could stand beside a naked woman and be tempted by a fruit?

"What's going on here, people?" asks the officer.

"I'm making love to my wife," the man answers indignantly.

"Oh, I'm sorry," says the cop. "I didn't know."

"Well," replies the man, "neither did I until you shined that light in her face."

Air Canada Flight

A man boards an Air Canada flight to Edmonton and takes his assigned seat. As he settles in, he glances up and sees a gorgeous woman walking down the aisle. He soon realizes she is heading straight toward his seat. Lo and behold, she takes the seat right next to his. Eager to strike up a conversation with her, he blurts out, "Business trip or vacation?"

The woman turns, smiles and says, "Business. I'm going to the Annual Nymphomaniac Convention."

The man swallows hard. Here is the most beautiful woman he has ever seen sitting next to him, and she is going to a meeting for nymphomaniacs! Struggling to maintain his composure, he calmly asks, "What's your business role at this convention?"

"Lecturer," she replies. "I use my experience to debunk some of the popular myths about sexuality."

"Really?" he says. "And what myths are those?"

"Well," she explains, "one popular myth is that American men are the most well endowed when, in fact, it's Native Canadian men who are most likely to possess that trait. Another popular myth is that French men are the best lovers, when actually it is the men of Jewish descent. We have, however, found that the best potential lover in all categories is the Alberta redneck."

Suddenly, the woman becomes a little uncomfortable and blushes. "I'm sorry," she says, "I really shouldn't be discussing this with you. I don't even know your name."

"Tonto," the man says. "Tonto Goldstein. But my friends call me 'Bubba.'"

Fur Guy

A middle-aged man walks into a posh downtown Toronto furrier with a gorgeous young blonde on his arm. "Show the lady your finest mink!" the fellow exclaims.

Q: Why did the Liberal politician close his eyes during sex?

A: Because he didn't want to see a woman disappointed.

The shop owner goes to the back of the store and returns with an absolutely gorgeous full-length mink coat. While the woman is trying on the coat, the furrier sidles up to the guy and discreetly whispers, "Ah, sir, that particular coat goes for $65,000."

"No problem! I'll write you a cheque!"

"Very good, sir," says the shop owner. "Today is Saturday. You may come by on Monday to pick up the coat, after the cheque has cleared."

On Monday afternoon, the fellow returns to the store.

The store owner is outraged. "How dare you show your face in here! There wasn't a single penny in your bank account!"

Q: Who would win in a fight between Celine Dion and Shania Twain?

A: We all would!

"I just had to come by," the guy replies, with a big smile on his face. "I wanted to thank you for the most wonderful weekend of my life!"

A Simple Discussion

Three middle-aged women are talking about their love lives over coffee at a local Tim Hortons in Saskatoon.

The first woman says, "My husband is like a Rolls Royce—smooth and sophisticated."

"Mine is like a Porsche—fast and powerful," says the second woman.

The third woman says, "Mine is like an old Chevy—it needs a hand start, and I have to jump on while it's still going."

The Birds, the Bees and Spiders

A father is in his backyard in Calgary watching his young daughter play in the garden. He smiles as he reflects on how sweet and innocent she is. Suddenly, she stops playing and stares at the ground. The father walks over to her and notices she is looking at two spiders.

"Daddy, what are those two spiders doing?" she asks.

"They're mating," her father replies.

"What do you call the spider on top, Daddy?" she asks.

"That's a Daddy Longlegs," her father says.

"So, the other one is Mommy Longlegs?" says the little girl.

"No," her father replies. "Both of them are Daddy Longlegs."

The little girl thinks for a moment, then lifts her foot and stomps both spiders flat. "Well, it might be okay in Québec or the Maritimes, but we're not having any of that shit in Alberta!"

Upright Fellows

Good friends Stu and Leroy are sitting in a bar in Prince George discussing popular trends on sex, marriage and family values.

Stu says, "I didn't have sex with my wife before we got married. How about you?"

Leroy replies, "I'm not sure. What was her maiden name?"

Golf Honeymoon

A couple is on their honeymoon in Niagara Falls when the husband confesses a secret to his new wife.

"Darling, I'm a golf addict," he says. "You'll never see me on the weekends, and all our vacations will be at golfing resorts."

"I've got a confession, too," replies the new wife, blushing. "I'm a hooker."

"That's not a problem," replies the husband. "Just keep your head down and your arms straight,"

Poor Wifey

A married woman in Winnipeg is having an affair with a TV repairman.

One afternoon while they are lying together on her couch, she says to him, "My husband never pays any attention to me. All he does is watch the latest basketball game on TV. That's why we've got the biggest HDTV in the city, just so he can watch all the games."

While she is complaining to the repairman, she hears the key in the front door. Her husband has arrived home early from work unexpectedly. She says to her lover, "Quick! Hide behind the TV!"

The repairman hides behind the big TV while the husband gets a beer and sits down to watch the basketball game. After 30 minutes, it becomes painful for the repairman to squat behind the TV any longer so he simply steps out, walks straight past the husband and out the front door.

The husband turns to his wife and says, "Hey, honey, I didn't see the referee send that guy off, did you?"

Decisions, Decisions

A rich bachelor in Ottawa is in love with three women and can't decide which one he should marry, so he decides to give each of them $200,000 to see how they handle the money.

Three months later, he asks each of them what they did with their share of the money.

The first woman proudly tells him that she invested her money in the TSX and that her portfolio had doubled in just three months.

The second woman explains that she set up a trust fund with her money and that it will ultimately grow and provide an endless source of funding for one of the young bachelor's favourite charities.

The third woman explains that she used her money as a down payment on a condo in the Caribbean so that they could escape the cold Canadian winters.

So in the end, which one of the women did the rich bachelor marry?

Why, the one with the biggest boobs of course!

Anybody There?

Once upon a time, a female brain cell happened to end up in a man's head by mistake.

She looks around nervously, but it is all empty and quiet.

"Hello?" she cries, but she gets no answer.

"Is there anyone here?" she says a little louder but still gets no answer.

Now, the female brain cell starts to feel alone and scared, and again she yells, "Hello! Is there anyone here?!"

Then she hears a voice from far, far away: "Hel-loooooo! We're down here!"

Artistic Tastes

A middle-aged couple in Victoria goes to a local art gallery. They come across a painting of a naked woman with only her privates covered with leaves. The wife doesn't like it and moves on, but her husband doesn't budge.

The wife turns around and asks, "What are you waiting for?"

The husband replies, "Autumn."

Magic

An Edmonton man having trouble achieving an erection decides to consult a witch doctor as a last resort.

The witch doctor throws some herbs on a fire, shakes the rattle in his hand and says, "I have placed a powerful spell on you, but it will work only once a year. Just say 'one, two, three,' and you'll get the largest erection you've ever had. After your wife has been satisfied, simply say 'one, two, three, four,' and it will disappear for 12 months."

Later that night as the man is lying in bed with his wife watching television, he says, "Watch this! One, two, three!" His penis becomes larger and stiffer than ever before.

His wife is amazed. She smiles and says, "That's great! But what did you say 'one, two, three' for?"

Hot Frenchie

During a heat wave one summer in Québec City, Pierre is taking a cold shower to cool off. When he gets out of the shower, he says to his wife, "It's just too hot to wear clothes today, honey. What do you think the neighbours would think if I mowed the lawn like this?"

"Probably that I married you for your money."

Kindness

A guy from Toronto takes a trip to Montréal. While there, he hires a prostitute. After sex, the prostitute says, "100 dollars."

The guy hands her $200.

The prostitute responds, "You're so kind!"

Some days pass, and the guy meets up with the same prostitute and has sex again.

The prostitute asks for $100, but the guy says, "No, here's $200."

The prostitute says, "You're so kind."

Two more days pass, and the guy hooks up with the prostitute one last time to have sex.

After they have sex, the prostitute says, "$100, please."

The guy hands her $200.

The prostitute says, "You're so kind. Where are you from?"

He answers, "I'm from Toronto."

The prostitute says, "I'm from there too!"

"I know," the guy replies. "Your mom sent me to give you $600."

Murder Motive

A man from rural Québec is on trial for killing his wife after he finds her in their bed with a neighbour. When the man is asked why he shot his wife instead of her lover, the man replies, "Ah, m'sieur, is it not better to shoot a woman once than a different man every week?"

In the Park

An old man walking through a park in Halifax spots a beautiful young woman suntanning on the grass. He walks up to her and says, "I want to feel your breasts!"

"Get away from me, you crazy old man!" the woman replies.

"I want to feel your breasts. I will give you $20," the old man says.

"Twenty dollars! Are you nuts? Get away from me!"

"I want to feel your breasts. I will give you $100!" he states.

"No! Get away from me!"

"$200," says the old man.

The young woman pauses to think about the offer, but then comes to her senses and says, "I said no!"

"I'll give you $500 if you let me feel your breasts," he says.

The woman takes a few moments to think it over...*Well, he is old, and he seems harmless enough. And $500 is a lot of money.* She finally says, "Well, okay, but only for a minute."

She gets up and loosens her bikini top, and while both are standing there on the grass, he slides his hands underneath and begins to feel her breasts. Then he starts saying, "Oh, my goodness. Oh, my goodness. Oh, my goodness..." while he is caressing the woman.

Out of curiosity, she asks him, "Why do you keep saying, 'Oh, my goodness. Oh, my goodness'?"

While continuing to feel her breasts, the old man replies, "Oh, my goodness. Oh, my goodness. Oh, my goodness…where am I ever going to get $500?"

Happiness

A Frenchman, an Italian and a Canadian are seated next to each other on an overseas flight. After a few cocktails, the men begin discussing their home lives.

"Last night I made love to my wife four times," the Frenchman brags, "and this morning she made me delicious crepes and told me how much she adores me."

"Ah, last night," the Italian says, "I made love to my wife six times, and this morning she made me a wonderful omelette and told me she could never love another man."

When the Canadian remains silent, the Frenchman smugly asks, "And how many times did you make love to your wife last night?"

"Once," he replies.

"Only once!" says the Italian, arrogantly snorting while the Frenchman laughs. "And what did she say to you this morning?"

"She said, 'I guess we had better stop—it's time to get up.'"

CHAPTER SIX
A Canadian on the Job

Whatcha Sellin'?

Two guys have just closed down their store on busy Yonge Street and are standing in the middle of their empty shop when one says to the other, "I'll bet you 10 bucks that if we wait here a few minutes, some Newfie is going to come by, peer through the window and come in and ask us what we're selling."

Sure enough, just as he finishes speaking, a Newfie sticks his face up to the window, looks around at the empty shelves and then walks in. "How's she goin, b'y? I was just wonderin' what you fellas was sellin'?"

One of the guys grins at the other and says, "We're selling idiots, sir."

The Newfie replies, "Well, ya must be doin' some good business 'cause dere's only two o' ya left."

Ditch Diggin'

A black guy, a Jewish guy and an Alberta redneck are digging a ditch at a construction site. The black guy's shovel hits something. He picks it up and sees that it's a lamp. He starts to rub the dirt off, and a genie pops out.

The genie says, "I will give each one of you a single wish. But choose carefully."

The black guy says, "I want my own country where all my brothers and sisters can live in peace and harmony forever."

The genie nods his head says, "Done," and the black guy is instantly transported to his new country.

The genie then turns to the Jewish guy. "What about you? What is your wish?"

The Jewish guy says, "I want my own country so the Jews can live in peace, free from war and persecution."

The genie says, "Done," and the Jewish guy magically disappears off to his new homeland.

Then the genie turns to the Alberta redneck and says, "What about you?"

The redneck says, "Now, let me get this straight. The blacks are all gonna live in their own country, and the Jews have their own country?"

"That's right," says the genie.

The redneck says, "In that case, make my woman's boobs bigger and fix my truck—we're goin' celebrating tonight!"

Diligent Surgeon

Michael Smith of Timmins, Ontario, is afflicted with a certain medical condition that necessitates he undergo a peculiarly delicate operation that involves the temporary removal of his testicles.

The chief surgeon at the hospital is performing the delicate surgery. After removing the patient's testicles and placing them ever so gently in a bowl beside the operating table, he is called out by a nurse for an emergency, leaving poor Mr. Smith alone in the room.

While the doctor is absent, and the patient is still under the influence of the anesthetic, the infirmary cat wanders into the room. The cat is normally confined to another ward, but it somehow managed to escape as cats tend to do.

Well, the mischievous feline jumps up on the table beside Mr. Smith and sees two round objects sitting in the bowl. After taking a sniff, the cat swiftly gobbles them up and bolts from the room.

Just then, the surgeon returns to his still unconscious patient. Imagine the surgeon's anguish when he looks into the bowl and discovers that his patient's testicles are missing!

Frantically, he looks around the room, on the floor and checks the table for the testicles. He even feels Mr. Smith's scrotum to see if someone has returned them. In a state of panic, the surgeon knows he can't simply sew Mr. Smith up with an empty sack. He could lose his medical licence and face severe judicial punishment for his mistake.

Time is quickly running out before the patient will wake up, so the surgeon tears apart the room looking for a suitable replacement, but all he can find are the two small onions his wife packed for his lunch. The surgeon finishes the operation just in time, and Mr. Smith recovers and leaves the hospital.

Several months later, the surgeon happens to run into his former patient on the street. "Hello, Mr. Smith! How are you feeling nowadays?" the surgeon asks with genuine interest.

Mr. Smith says with a big smile on his face, "Why, doc, I'm feeling fantastic! Thank you!"

The doctor lets out a sigh of relief.

"It would seem I'm cured, eh," adds Mr. Smith. "However, there's one thing I wish you'd explain to me. How is it that every time I need to take a piss, my eyes begin to water?"

Relocation

An executive of a large corporation in Thunder Bay is told that he must relocate to a new position at the head office in Toronto.

The executive tells his boss that he would rather quit his job than move to the big city. "There's so much crime and so many senseless murders there," the executive whines. "I'm worried about the safety of my wife and kids. It's scary there. All you hear about on the news are the shootings and rapes that happen in that city."

The boss tries to console the man by telling him that he lived in Toronto once and that there are many positive aspects to the city. He tells him about the great restaurants, nightlife and transportation. "I lived there for 10 years, and I never once felt threatened," says the boss.

A CANADIAN ON THE JOB   101

"What kind of work did you do there?" asks the executive.

"I worked for the NHL."

"What did you do for the NHL?" asks the executive.

The boss replies, "I was the tail gunner on Gary Bettman's limousine."

A Real Hero

A mine near a small town in northern Manitoba completely collapses. One of the engineers who miraculously survived the disaster goes into the local watering hole a few weeks later. The bar is empty except for one lonely soul at the other end of the bar.

"Hey, bartender," says the engineer. "I'll have a beer, and pour another one for my friend down at the end there."

The bartender says, "I'm sorry, sir, but that guy's a commie, and we don't serve his kind around here."

"Well, you'd better, because if it weren't for that guy, I wouldn't be here! You remember that mine that caved in? Well, I was in that mine, and so was that guy. When the last of us were escaping, he held the roof of the mine up with his head! So get him a beer, and if you don't believe me, look at the top of his head, and you'll see that it's flat from holding the roof up."

The bartender skeptically serves the commie his beer and then goes back to talk to the engineer. "I saw the flat spot on his head," says the bartender, "but I also couldn't help noticing the bruising under his chin. What is that all about?"

The engineer replies, "Oh...that's where we put the jack."

Ambulance Service

A Vancouver prostitute finishes working the night shift, gets into her car and starts to drive back to her apartment. On the way there, she is involved in a serious car crash. The paramedics arrive soon after, drag her out of the car and lay her on the ground to examine her.

Medic: "Okay, Miss, I'm going to check if you're concussed."

Prostitute: "Okay..."

Medic: "How many fingers am I putting up?"

Prostitute: "Oh no! I'm paralyzed from the waist down!"

Sick of Work

Sam has been in the computer business for 25 years and is sick of the stress and the rat race of the big city. He quits his job in Toronto and buys a section of land in northern Ontario as far away from humanity as possible. Sam sees the postman once a week and gets groceries once a month. Otherwise, it's total peace and quiet. After six months or so of almost total isolation, he's just finishing dinner one evening when someone knocks on his door. He opens it and sees a big bearded man standing there.

"Name's Leon, your neighbour from four kilometres south of here. Having a party Saturday and thought you'd like to come."

"Great!" says Sam. "After six months out here, I'm ready to meet some local folks. Thank you."

As Leon is leaving, he stops, turns around and says, "Gotta warn you; there's gonna be some drinkin'."

"No problem," replies Sam. "After 25 years in the computer business, I can drink with the best of 'em."

Again, as Leon starts to leave, he stops and says, "More 'n' likely gonna be some fightin' too."

Sam says, "Well, I get along with people. I'll be there. Thanks again."

Once again, Leon turns from the door and says, "Might be some wild sex at the party too."

"Now that's not a problem, either," says Sam. "I've been all alone for six months! I'll definitely be there! By the way, what should I wear?"

Leon replies, "Whatever you want—just gonna be the two of us."

Oops!

A restaurant is opening a new location in downtown Saskatoon, and one of the owner's friends sends flowers for the occasion. However, when the owner reads the card with the flowers, it says, "Rest in Peace." The owner is a little peeved, and he calls the florist right away to complain.

After he tells the florist about the obvious mistake, the florist says, "Sir, I'm really sorry for the mistake, but rather than getting angry, you should imagine this: somewhere there is a funeral taking place today, and the flowers will have a note saying, 'Congratulations on Your New Location!'"

Canadian Workers

A Canadian businessman is showing his machine factory to a potential customer from Russia. At noon, when the lunch whistle blows, 2000 men and women immediately stop work and leave the building.

"Your workers—they're escaping!" cries the Russian visitor. "You must stop them!"

"Don't worry. They'll be back," replies the Canadian. And indeed, at exactly one o'clock, the whistle blows again, and all the workers return from their lunch break.

When the tour is over, the Canadian manufacturer turns to his guest and says, "Well, now, which of these machines would you like to order?"

"Forget the machines," says the visitor. "How much do you want for that whistle?"

Barn Life

Three men are travelling in rural Saskatchewan when their car breaks down, whereupon they seek shelter at the nearest farmhouse.

The farmer has only two spare beds, and, of course, his daughter's, but since he has heard bad stories about strangers, he informs the men that one of them will have to sleep in the barn. One of the men, a polite Hindu mathematician, immediately volunteers and goes out to the barn.

A short time later, there is a knock on the door, and the Hindu apologizes and explains that there are cows in the barn, and because of his religious convictions, he doesn't think he can sleep there.

Q: What happens to a lawyer when he takes Viagra?
A: He gets taller.

A second man, a conservative rabbi, volunteers to sleep in the barn. A short time later, there is a knock on the door. It is the rabbi, who explains that since there is a pig in the barn, he isn't comfortable staying in the barn.

Whereupon the third man, a practicing lawyer, agreeably proceeds out to the barn.

In a little while, there is another knock on the door. And when the farmer answers it, sure enough, there are the cows and the pig.

Fries, Anyone?

A sheep farmer in New Zealand needs help with the difficult task of castrating some of his inferior male sheep to keep them from breeding with the females.

He hires a travelling French Canadian guy who doesn't speak much English but says he is a good worker. After the first day, the two men successfully castrate 14 sheep, and when the French worker is just about to throw away the "parts," the sheep farmer yells, "No! Don't throw those away! My wife fries them up and we eat them. We call them 'sheep fries,' and they're delicious."

Later that day, the French hired hand comes in for supper, and indeed the sheep fries are tasty. The next day, they castrate 16 sheep, and later on they all settle down to another supper of sheep fries.

On the third day, however, when the sheep farmer returns home from running errands, he asks his wife where the French hired hand is, and she says, "You know, it's the weirdest thing! I told him since there aren't very many sheep fries this evening, we were also going to have French fries, and he ran like hell!"

Good Doggie!

In Ottawa, a guy sees a sign in front of a house:
Talking Dog for Sale.

He rings the bell, and the owner tells him the dog is in the backyard. The guy goes to the backyard and sees a black mutt just sitting there.

"You talk?" he asks.

"Sure do," says the dog.

"So, what's your story?"

The dog looks up and says, "Well, I discovered my gift of speech pretty young, and I wanted to help the government, so I told the Canadian Armed Forces, and in no time they were jetting me from country to country, sitting in rooms with spies and world leaders, because no one figured a dog could eavesdrop. I was one of their most valuable spies eight years running. But the jetting around really tired me out, and I knew I wasn't getting any younger and I wanted to settle down. So I signed up for a job at the airport to do some undercover security work, mostly wandering near suspicious characters and listening in. I uncovered some incredible dealings and was awarded a bunch of medals. I then had a wife and a mess of puppies and now I'm just retired."

The guy is amazed. He goes back in the house and asks the owner how much he wants for the dog.

The owner says, "Ten dollars."

"That dog is amazing," replies the man. "Why on earth are you selling him so cheaply?"

"'Cause he's a liar!" replies the dog owner. "He didn't do any of that stuff!"

Newfie Reporter

A car is involved in an accident on a busy street in St. John's. As expected, a large group of curious onlookers gathers around the area. A Newfie newspaper reporter arrives on the scene and is anxious to get his story but can't get near the car because of all the people.

Being a clever sort, he starts shouting loudly, "Let me through! Let me through! I'm the son of the victim!"

The crowd makes way for the Newfie to get through.

Lying in front of the car is a donkey.

The Tour Guide

Rocky Mountain guides who always do the same trails can get tired of answering the same questions over and over. One time during a tour, an American tourist is giving his guide an especially hard time with silly questions. They are walking through a mountain valley that is strewn with rocks, and the traveller asks, "How did these rocks get here?"

"Sir," replies the guide, "they were brought down by a glacier."

The tourist peers up the mountain and says, "But I don't see any glacier."

"Oh, really?" replies the guide. "I guess it went back for more rocks."

City Slicker

Chuck has lived in Toronto all his life and is tired of the rat race, so he decides to give up the city life and move to the country to become a chicken farmer. As it turns out, his neighbour, George, is also a chicken farmer.

George goes to visit Chuck one day and says, "Chicken farming ain't easy. Tell you what. To help you get started, I'll give you 100 chickens."

Chuck is thrilled by George's generosity. Two weeks later, George drops by to see how things are going. The new farmer says, "Not too well. All 100 chickens died."

George replies, "Oh, I can't believe that. I've never had any trouble with my chickens. I'll give you 100 more."

Another two weeks go by, and George stops by Chuck's again. The new farmer says, "You're not going to believe this, but the second batch of 100 chickens died too."

Astounded by this news, George asks, "What went wrong?"

The new farmer replies, "Well, I'm not sure whether I'm planting them too deep or too close together."

Ten Best Excuses for When You Get Caught Falling Asleep at Your Desk

10. "They told me at the blood bank this might happen."

9. "This is just a 15-minute power-nap like they raved about in that time-management course you sent me to."

8. "Whew! Guess I left the top off the White-Out. You probably got here just in time!"

7. "I wasn't sleeping! I was meditating on the mission statement and envisioning a new paradigm."

6. "I was testing my keyboard for drool resistance."

5. "I was doing a highly specific yoga exercise to relieve work-related stress. Are you discriminatory toward people who practice yoga?"

4. "Why did you interrupt me? I had almost figured out a solution to our biggest problem."

3. "The coffee machine is broken."

2. "Someone must have put decaf in the wrong pot."

And the number one best thing to say if you get caught sleeping at your desk...

1. "...in Jesus' name. Amen."

Bill Gates

I was in the airport VIP lounge en route to Toronto a couple of weeks ago. I noticed Bill Gates sitting comfortably at a table in the corner, enjoying a drink. I was meeting a VIP who was also flying to Toronto, but she was running a little bit late. Well, being a straightforward kind of guy, I approached the Microsoft chairman, introduced myself and said, "Mr. Gates, I wonder if you would do me a favour?"

"Yes?"

"I'm sitting right over there," I said, pointing to my seat at the bar, "and I'm waiting on a very important client. Would you be so kind when she arrives as to walk by and just say, 'Hi, Mark'?"

"Sure."

I shook his hand, thanked him and went back to my seat.

About 10 minutes later, my client shows up. We order a drink and start to talk business. A couple of minutes later, I feel a tap on my shoulder. It's Bill Gates of course.

"Hi, Mark," he says.

I reply, "Get lost, Gates, I'm in a meeting."

Pilot Error

A huge Air Canada jumbo jet is just coming into Pearson Airport in Toronto on its final approach. The pilot says over the intercom, "Hello. This is Captain Johnson. We're on our final descent into Toronto. I want to take this opportunity to thank you for flying with Air Canada today, and I hope you enjoy your stay in Toronto."

After that greeting, the pilot forgets to switch off the intercom. All the passengers can now hear the conversation taking place in the cockpit.

The co-pilot says to the pilot, "Well, captain, whatcha gonna do in Toronto?"

"Well," replies the captain, "first I'm gonna check into the hotel and go for a mega-huge dump. Then I'm gonna take that new flight attendant out for supper—you know, the one with the huge tits. I'm gonna wine and dine her, take her back to my room and slip the old salami to her all night."

Well, everyone on the plane is now trying to get a look at the new flight attendant. She's so embarrassed that she runs from the back of the plane to try to get to the cockpit to turn the intercom off.

Halfway down the aisle, the flight attendant trips on an old lady's purse, and down she goes.

The old lady leans over and says to the flight attendant, "No need to run, dearie, he's got to go for a shit first!"

The Perfect Employee

In a small town in eastern Canada, there is a rather sizeable factory that hires only married men.

Concerned about this, a local woman calls the manager and asks him, "Why is it you limit your employees to married men? Is it because you think women are weak, dumb, cantankerous or what?"

"Not at all, ma'am," the manager replies. "It's because our employees are used to obeying orders, are accustomed to being shoved around, know how to keep their mouths shut and don't pout when I yell at them."

Pickle Factory

There was a man who worked his whole life at an Etobicoke pickle factory. One day he comes home and tells his wife that he has just been fired from his job.

His wife starts to scream and yell. "You have given them 20 years of devoted service. Why did they fire you?"

"For 20 years I've wanted to stick my pecker in the pickle slicer," he explained, "and today I finally did it!"

The wife runs over to her husband and pulls his pants down to see what damage has been done.

"You look okay," she says with a sigh of relief. "So what happened to the pickle slicer?"

"Well," he says with hesitation, "they fired her, too."

Signs that You've Had too Much at the Office Christmas Party

1. You notice your tie sticking out of your fly.
2. Someone uses your tongue for a coaster.
3. You start kissing the portraits of the prime ministers on the wall.
4. You see your gonch hanging from the light fixture in the ceiling.
5. You have to hold on to the floor to keep from sliding off.
6. You strike a match and light your nose.
7. You take off your shoes and wade in the potato salad.
8. You hear someone say, "Call a priest!"
9. You hear a duck quacking, and it's you.
10. You complain about the small bathroom after emerging from the closet.

New Hire

A company is looking to hire someone for an important position, so they interview dozens of applicants. They narrow the search down to three men from different parts of Canada.

In an attempt to pick one of them, the company decides to ask the applicants all the same question, which they have 24 hours to answer, and the one with the best answer will get the job.

Here is the question:

"A man and a woman are in bed, nude. The woman is lying on her side with her back facing the man, and the man is lying on his side facing the woman's back. What is the man's name?"

After the 24 hours are up, the three applicants are brought in to give their answers.

The first man, from Montréal, says, "My answer is...there *is* no answer."

The second man, from Hamilton, says, "My answer is...there is no way to determine the answer with the information we were given."

The third applicant, from Newfoundland, says, "I'm not exactly sure, but I've narrowed it down to two names. It's either 'Willie Turner' or 'Willie Nailer.'"

The Newfoundlander got the job.

Good Advice

An experienced Air Canada pilot to a nervous passenger: "You think you are afraid to fly. But in reality, you're afraid to fall."

Overheard at a Software Help Centre

Company help desk clerk: "What's on your monitor now, ma'am?"

Customer: "A teddy bear my boyfriend bought for me at the supermarket."

Help Wanted

A man applies for a job. After filling out the application, he waits anxiously for the outcome. The employer looks over his application and says, "We have an opening for people like you."

"Oh, great," the man says. "What is it?"

"It's called the door!"

Ding Dong, Avon Calling

An Avon lady delivering beauty products to customers in a high-rise in downtown Toronto is riding in the elevator. Suddenly, she has the powerful urge to fart. Since no one is in the elevator with her, she lets it go—and it is a doozy.

The elevator then stops at the next floor, so she quickly uses some Avon Pine-Scented Spray to cover up the smell. A man enters the elevator and immediately makes a face. "Holy cow!" he exclaims. "What's that smell?"

"I don't know, sir. I don't smell anything," replies the Avon lady. "What does it smell like to you?"

"Like someone crapped a Christmas tree."

CHAPTER SEVEN

A Canadian Abroad

Strolling Through the Park

A Canadian couple is strolling through a park in London, England. They stop and sit down on a bench next to an elderly Brit. The Brit notices their lapel pins sporting the Canadian flag and, to make conversation, he says, "Judging by your pins, you must be Canadians."

"Indeed we are," replies the Canadian man.

"I hope you won't mind my asking," says the Brit, "but what do the two red bars on your flag represent?"

"Well," replies the Canadian man, "one of the bars stands for the courage and hardiness of our people in settling the cold and broad prairies of our country. The other is for the honesty and integrity for which Canadians are known."

The Brit mulls this over and nods. Having poor eyesight at his advanced age, and not being familiar with maple leaves, he then asks, "And what's that six-pointed item in the middle of your flag?"

"Oh, that's to remind us of the six words of our national motto," the Canadian woman pipes up.

The Brit asks, "And what are those six words?"

The Canadian woman smiles and replies, "They are 'Don't blame us—we're not Americans.'"

A Newfie on Vacation

A Newfie is staying at a fancy hotel in Miami and is enjoying the outdoor swimming pool when the manager tells him quite bluntly to get out.

When asked for the reason, the manager says, "Because you peed in the pool."

"Well," replies the Newfie, "lots of people do that."

"True," answers the manager, "but you did it while standing on the damn diving board!"

In Trouble

A Canadian hockey fan, an American hockey fan and a Swedish hockey fan are in a hotel room in Saudi Arabia sharing a smuggled case of beer. All of a sudden, the Saudi police rush in and arrest them. The mere possession of alcohol is a severe offence in Saudi Arabia, so for the terrible crime of consuming alcohol, they are sentenced to death!

However, after many months and with the help of excellent lawyers, the three hockey fans successfully appeal their sentence down to life imprisonment.

By a stroke of luck, it is a Saudi national holiday the day when their trial finishes, and the extremely benevolent sheik decides to release the men after each receives 20 lashes with a whip.

As they are preparing for their punishment, the sheik suddenly says, "It's my first wife's birthday today, and she has asked me to allow each of you one wish before your flogging."

The Swede fan is first in line (he had drunk the least), so he thinks for a while and then says, "Please tie a pillow to my back." This is done, but the pillow only lasts 10 lashes before the whip goes through. The Swedish fan is carried away bleeding and crying with pain when the punishment is done.

The American fan is next up (he finished four beer), and after watching the scene with the Swedish fan, says, "All right! Please place two pillows on my back." But the two pillows only take 15 lashes before the whip goes through again. The American fan is carried away crying.

The Canadian fan is the last one up (he had the most beer), but before he can say anything, the sheik turns to him and says, "You support the greatest team in the world and your country has the best and most loyal hockey fans in the world. For this, you may have two wishes!"

"Thanks, your most Royal Highness," the Canadian replies. "In recognition of your kindness, my first wish is that you give me not 20 but 100 lashes."

"Not only are you an honourable, handsome and powerful man, but you are also very brave," the sheik says with an admiring look on his face. "If 100 lashes is what you desire, then so be it. And your second wish? What is it to be?" the sheik asks.

"Tie the American to my back."

Return Home

A man from Québec returns home after a trip to Florida and passes through Canadian Customs. The customs official asks the standard question: "Have you anything to declare?"

The Frenchman thinks for a second and finally says, "It's a nice day."

Off to Rome

A Calgarian is getting a haircut before taking a trip to Rome with his wife.

He mentions the trip to the barber, who responds, "Rome? Why would anyone want to go there? It's crowded, dirty and full of Italians. You're crazy to go to Rome. So, what airline are you using?"

"We're taking Air Canada," replies the man. "We got a great deal!"

"Air Canada!" exclaims the barber. "That's a terrible airline. Their planes are old, their flight attendants are rude and they're always late. So, where are you staying in Rome?"

"We'll be at the downtown International Marriott."

"That dump! That's the worst hotel in the city," says the barber. "The rooms are small, the service is surly and they're overpriced. So, whatcha gonna do when you get there?"

"We're going to see the Vatican, and we hope to see the Pope."

"That's rich!" says the barber with a laugh. "You and a million other people trying to see him. He'll look the size of an ant. Boy, good luck on this lousy trip of yours. You're going to need it."

A month later, the man again comes in for his regular haircut. The barber asks him about his trip to Rome.

"It was wonderful," replies the man. "Not only did we fly in one of Air Canada's brand-new airplanes, but the flight was overbooked so they bumped us up to first class. The food and wine were delicious, and I had a beautiful young flight attendant who waited on me hand and foot. And the hotel—it was great! They'd just finished a $25-million remodelling job, and now it's the finest hotel in the city. The hotel was also overbooked, so they apologized and gave us the presidential suite at no extra charge!"

"Well," mutters the barber, "I know you didn't get to see the Pope."

"Actually, we were quite lucky, because as we toured the Vatican, a Swiss Guard tapped me on the shoulder and explained that the Pope likes to personally meet some of the visitors, and if I'd be so kind as to step into his private room and wait, the Pope would personally greet us. Sure enough, five minutes later, the Pope walks through the door and shakes my hand! I knelt down and he spoke to me."

"Really?" asks the barber. "What'd he say?"

"He said, 'Where'd you get the lousy haircut?'"

Travelling Salesman

"Selling abroad can be difficult," a salesman explains to his friend. "When I got sent to the Middle East, I was confident that I could make a good sales pitch as cola is virtually unknown there. But I had a problem—I didn't know how to speak Arabic. So I planned to convey the message through three posters. The first poster showed a man crawling through the hot desert sand, totally exhausted and almost fainting. The second poster was of the same man drinking our cola. The final poster was of the man now totally refreshed. These posters were pasted all over the place."

"That should have worked," says the friend.

"Well, not only did I not speak Arabic," says the salesman, "but I also didn't realize that Arabs read from right to left."

Love thy Neighbour

An Englishman, Frenchman, American and Canadian are flying across Canada on a small plane when the pilot makes an announcement: "We're having mechanical problems, and the only way we can make it to the closest airport is for three of you to open the door and jump so that at least one of you can survive."

The four men open the door and look down below. The Englishman takes a deep breath and hollers, "God save the Queen!" and jumps.

The Frenchman gets really inspired and hollers, "Viva la France!" and he also jumps out of the plane.

This really pumps up the Canadian, so he hollers, "Remember 1812!" and he grabs the American and throws him out of the plane.

Another Newfie on Vacation

A young Newfie woman is on vacation in Louisiana. She wants to buy a pair of genuine alligator shoes in the worst way, but she's reluctant to pay the high prices the local vendors are asking.

After becoming frustrated with the "no haggle" attitude of one of the shopkeepers, the Newfie shouts, "Maybe I'll just go out and catch my own alligator so I can get a pair of shoes at a reasonable price!"

The shopkeeper says, "By all means, be my guest. Maybe you'll luck out and catch yourself a big one!"

Determined, the woman heads for the swamps, set on catching herself an alligator.

Later in the day, the shopkeeper is driving home when he spots the young woman standing waist deep in the water, shotgun in hand. He also sees a huge nine-foot alligator swimming quickly toward her. She takes aim, kills the creature and with a great deal of effort, hauls it onto the swamp bank. Lying nearby are several more of the dead creatures.

The shopkeeper watches in amazement.

Just then, the Newfie flips the alligator on its back, and clearly frustrated, she shouts out, "Shit! This one ain't wearing any shoes either!"

American Visit

A blind Canadian tourist travels to Texas by bus. He gets off the bus in Fort Worth and asks the person next to him, "Excuse me. Can you tell me where's a good place to eat?"

A woman says, "Right down the road is a men's club."

The blind man doesn't realize the club also has a swimming pool, a workout room and a racquetball court. He just finds his way to the restaurant and is directed to a table. He says to the waitress, "Please bring me a steak and a Coke."

The waitress brings him a mug that is 12 inches in diameter and over a foot tall. The man says, "I just wanted a Coke, not the whole factory!"

The waitress says, "Mister, this is Texas; everything's bigger in Texas." She soon returns with his steak, and it hangs over all the sides of a huge sizzling platter.

The blind man says, "Lady, I just wanted a steak, not the whole cow!"

She replies, "Mister, this is Texas; everything's bigger in Texas."

He finally finishes his meal and asks the waitress, "Which way to the toilet?"

"It's just down the hall, third door on the right," she replies.

The man goes down the hall and absentmindedly opens the third door on the left and, with one step, falls into the club's swimming pool. "Help! Help!" he screams. "Please don't flush!"

Deadly Assassins

Two Canadian assassins are hired to kill a dictator in South America. For years the evil dictator has killed and tortured his own people and has threatened the security of the world. Governments around the globe have tried to kill him, but no one has been successful. Prime Minister Stephen Harper decides to get the best Canadian assassins, as no one in the world would expect a Canadian to be involved in an international plot to kill a dictator.

So after two months of briefing, the two assassins are flown secretly into the country to begin their work. They follow the dictator's every move for months and find out that every day at noon he goes outside and does stretching exercises.

The assassins set up shop right across the street, get all of their sights set, load their guns and have everything ready to go. It is now just a matter of time before the world is finally rid of the horrible dictator.

Noon comes, no dictator. Ten minutes later, no dictator.

One assassin turns to the other and says, "Gee, I hope nothing happened to him."

Language Test

A Swiss guy, looking for directions, pulls up at a bus stop where two Edmontonians are waiting.

"Entschuldigung, koennen Sie Deutsch sprechen?" says the Swiss guy. The two Canadians just stare at him.

"Excusez-moi. Parlez vous francais?" The two continue to stare.

"Parlare italiano?" No response.

"Hablan ustedes espanol?" Still nothing.

The Swiss guy drives off, extremely disgusted.

The first Canadian turns to the second and says, "Y'know, maybe we should learn a foreign language."

"Why?" replies the other. "That guy knew four languages, and it didn't do him any good."

Shipwrecked

After living his entire life in Winnipeg and never really living his life, a young single guy finally decides to take a trip on a cruise ship. He is having the time of his life when the ship slams into an iceberg and begins to sink. The guy manages to grab onto a piece of driftwood and, using his last ounce of strength, swims a few miles through the shark-infested sea to a remote island.

Sprawled on the shore and nearly passed out from exhaustion, he turns his head and sees a woman lying near him, unconscious, barely breathing. She also washed up on shore from the sinking ship. He crawls over to her, and with some mouth-to-mouth assistance, he manages to get her breathing again. She looks up at him, wide-eyed and grateful, and exclaims, "My God, you saved my life!"

He suddenly realizes the woman is the Victoria Secret supermodel Adriana Lima!

Days and weeks go by. The guy builds a hut for them to live in; there's fruit trees on the small island; and they're in heaven. Adriana falls madly in love with the man, and they make passionate love morning, noon and night.

Alas, one day she notices that her lover is looking kind of glum.

"What's the matter, sweetheart?" she asks. "We have a wonderful life together. I'm in love with you. Is there something wrong? Is there anything I can do?"

He says, "Actually, Adriana, there is. Would you mind putting on my shirt?"

"Sure," she says, "if it will help."

He takes off his shirt, and she puts it on.

"Now would you put on my pants?" he asks.

"Sure, honey, if it's really going to make you feel better," she says.

"Okay, would you put on my hat now and draw a little moustache on your face?" he asks.

"Whatever you want, sweetie," she says.

Then he says, "Now, would you start walking around the edge of the island?"

Adriana starts walking around the perimeter of the island. He sets off in the other direction. They meet up halfway around the island about 15 minutes later. He rushes up to her, grabs her by the shoulders and says, "Dude! You'll never believe who I'm sleeping with!"

Newfie Groom

A Newfie wants to marry a sheik's daughter in Egypt. So the sheik says to the Newfie, "You have to complete three tasks before you can marry her."

The Newfie replies, "That sounds good."

The sheik says, "There are three tents. In the first tent, there is a 40-ounce bottle of rum, which you have to drink in a half hour."

The Newfie replies, "Piece of cake."

"In the second tent," the sheik says, "there is a giant tiger that needs a tooth pulled."

The Newfie replies, "Easy."

"And in the third tent," the sheik says, "there is a woman who has never been sexually pleasured before, and you have to pleasure her."

The Newfie replies, "Not a problem."

So the Newfie goes into the first tent, and a half hour later, he walks out and says, "Well, that was easy enough. Bring on the next tent."

The Newfie staggers into the second tent, and a couple of seconds later, the tent starts to shake and strange noises are heard. A few minutes later, there is silence. The Newfie walks out of the tent, bleeding with his clothes ripped to shreds, and says, "Now, where's that woman who wants her tooth pulled?"

Pushy Salesman

As Canadian tourists in Israel, Morris and his wife are sitting outside a Bethlehem souvenir shop, waiting for their fellow travellers.

An Arab salesman carrying belts approaches the couple. After an impassioned sales talk yields no results, he asks where they are from.

"Canada," Morris replies.

Looking at the woman's dark hair and olive-coloured skin, the Arab says, "She's not from Canada."

"Yes, I am," says the wife.

The Arab looks at her again and asks, "Is he your husband?"

"Yes," she replies.

Turning to the husband, the Arab says, "I'll give you 100 camels for her."

Morris looks stunned, and after a long silence, he replies, "She's not for sale."

After the Arab leaves, the somewhat indignant wife says, "Morris, what took you so long to answer that salesman?"

Morris replies, "I was trying to figure out how to get 100 camels back home."

Ahhh, Japan

A Canadian businessman is in Japan. A few Japanese businessmen take him out, get him drunk and send him upstairs to his hotel room with a hooker.

As the Canadian is having sex with her, she starts screaming, "Nashagai ana! Nashagai ana!"

The man keeps going, saying, "Yeah, baby, take it all." He keeps pumping, and she keeps screaming, "Nashagai ana! Nashagai ana!"

The next day, the man is playing golf with one of the Japanese guys. The Canadian is hungover so he slices his ball, and it goes way off to the right. The Japanese businessman says, "Nashagai ana."

The Canadian says, "What does that mean?"

The Japanese man says, "Wrong hole."

Giggles

Two Canadian missionaries in Africa are kidnapped by a tribe of hostile cannibals who put the two men in a large pot of water, build a huge fire under it and leave them there. A few minutes later, one of the missionaries starts to laugh uncontrollably.

The other missionary can't believe it! He says, "What's wrong with you? We're being boiled alive! They're gonna eat us! What could possibly be funny at a time like this?"

The other missionary says, "I just peed in the soup."

Saudi Arabia

Three guys from Halifax are on a trip to Saudi Arabia. One day, they stumble into a harem tent filled with over 100 beautiful women. They start getting friendly with all the women, when suddenly, the sheik comes in.

"I am the master of all these women," the sheik says. "No one else can touch them except me. You men must pay for what you have done today. You will be punished in a way corresponding to your profession." He turns to the first man and asks him what he does for a living.

"I'm a police officer," says the first man.

"Then we will shoot your penis off!" says the sheik. He then turns to the second man and asks him what he does for a living.

"I'm a firefighter," the man replies.

"Then we will burn your penis off!" says the sheik. Finally, he asks the last man, "And you, what do you do for a living?"

The third man replies, "I'm a lollipop salesman!"

Finish?

A virile, middle-aged Italian gentleman named Guido is relaxing at his favourite bar in Rome. He sees a spectacular young blonde woman and strikes up a conversation with her.

Things progress to the point where he leads her back to his apartment and, after some small talk, they retire to his bedroom where he rattles her senseless. After a pleasant interlude, he asks with a smile, "So, you finish?"

The woman pauses for a second, frowns and replies, "No."

Surprised, Guido reaches for her and the rattling resumes. This time she thrashes about wildly and there are screams of passion. The sex finally ends and, again, Guido smiles and asks, "You finish?"

Again, after a short pause, she returns his smile, cuddles closer to him and softly says, "No."

Stunned, but damned if he is going to leave this woman unsatisfied, Guido reaches for the woman yet again. Using the last of his strength, he barely manages it, but they come together, screaming, bucking, clawing and ripping the bed sheets. Exhausted, Guido falls onto his back, gasping.

Barely able to turn his head, he looks into her eyes, smiles proudly and asks again, "You finish?"

Barely able to speak, the beautiful blonde whispers in his ear, "No, I Canadian."

Blood Lines

On a train from London to Manchester, a Canadian is telling off the Englishman sitting across from him.

"You English are too stuffy. You set yourselves apart too much. Look at me…in me, I have Italian blood, French blood, a little Native blood and some Swedish blood. What do you say to that?"

The Englishman replies, "Very sporting of your mother."

CHAPTER EIGHT

A Canadian at War and Peace

A Little Rest and Relaxation

A Canadian soldier serving in World War II has just returned from several weeks of intense action on the German front lines. He has finally been granted a few days of R&R and is in Southampton, England, to board a train bound for London.

The train is crowded, so the soldier walks the length of the train, looking for an empty seat. The only seat unoccupied is directly across from a well-dressed, middle-aged woman, and on the seat is her small dog.

The war-weary soldier says, "Please, ma'am, may I sit in that seat?"

The English woman looks down her nose at the soldier, sniffs and says, "You Canadians. You are such a rude class of people. Can't you see my little Fifi is using that seat?"

The soldier walks away, determined to find a place to rest, but after another trip down to the end of the train, he finds himself again facing the woman with the dog in the opposite seat.

Again he asks, "Please, lady. May I sit there? I'm very tired."

The English woman wrinkles her nose and snorts, "You Canadians! Not only are you rude, but you are also quite arrogant."

The soldier leans against the swaying wall of the train and again asks if he might please sit down.

The woman replies, "Not only are you Canadians rude and arrogant, but you're also very inconsiderate."

The soldier doesn't say anything else. He leans over, picks up the little dog and tosses it out the window of the train and sits down in the empty seat.

While the woman shrieks, demanding that someone defend her and chastise the soldier, an English gentleman sitting across the aisle speaks up, "You know, sir, you Canadians do seem to have a penchant for doing the wrong thing. You eat holding the fork in the wrong hand. You drive your autos on the wrong side of the road. And now, sir, you've thrown the wrong bitch out the window."

Lots of Action

An old but still ruggedly handsome sergeant major in the Royal Canadian Armed Forces finds himself at a gala event hosted by a local liberal arts college. There is no shortage of young, idealistic women in attendance, one of whom approaches the man for conversation. "Excuse me, Sergeant Major, but you seem to be a very serious man. Is something bothering you?"

"Negative, ma'am. Just serious by nature."

The young woman looks at his awards and decorations on his coat and says, "It looks like you have seen a lot of action."

"Yes, ma'am, a lot of action."

The young lady, tiring of trying to start up a conversation, says, "You know, you should lighten up a little. Relax and enjoy yourself."

The sergeant major just stares at her in his serious manner. Finally, the woman says, "You know, I hope you don't take this the wrong way, but when is the last time you had sex?"

"1955, ma'am."

"Well, there you are. You really need to chill out and quit taking everything so seriously! I mean, no sex since 1955!"

Q: Why don't Canadian women wear sleeveless dresses?
A: They aren't allowed to bare arms.

Feeling charitable and a little bit drunk, she takes his hand and leads him to a private room where she proceeds to "relax" him several times. Afterwards, panting for breath, she leans against his bare chest and says, "Wow, you sure didn't forget much since 1955!"

The sergeant major, glancing at his watch, says in his matter-of-fact voice, "I hope not—it's only 21:30 now."

Canadian Power

A brigade of Taliban soldiers are walking down a road when they hear a voice call from behind a sand dune: "One man from Canada is better than 10 Taliban."

The Taliban commander quickly orders 10 of his best men over the dune whereupon a gun battle breaks out and continues for a few minutes and then is followed by silence.

The voice once again calls out: "One man from Canada is better than 100 Taliban."

Furious, the Taliban commander sends his next best 100 troops over the dune and instantly a huge gunfight commences. After 10 minutes of battle, again, silence.

The rebel voice calls out again: "One man from Canada is better than 1000 Taliban."

The enraged Taliban commander musters 1000 fighters and sends them to the other side of the dune. Rifle fire, machine guns, grenades, rockets and cannon fire ring out as a terrible battle is fought. Then silence.

Eventually, one badly wounded Taliban fighter crawls back over the dune and with his dying words tells his commander, "Don't send any more men; it's a trap. There are two of them."

Under Attack

During World War II, the Japanese attack a Canadian warship. A torpedo is heading toward the ship, and a hit seems inevitable. The captain tells the navigator to run down to the crew quarters and tell a joke or something. At least they would die laughing.

The navigator goes down and says to the crew, "What would you think if I could split the whole ship in two by hitting my dick against the table?"

The crew bursts out laughing. So the navigator pulls his dick out and whams it on the table just as the torpedo hits. A huge explosion tears the ship apart.

The only survivors are the captain and the navigator. As they float around in a lifeboat, the captain asks the navigator, "Well, I heard the crew laugh right before the explosion. What did you do?"

The navigator tells him about how he hit his dick against the table.

The captain then says, "Well, in the future you'd better be careful with that dick of yours. The torpedo missed!"

Captain's Orders

A young, freshly minted lieutenant from Toronto is sent to Bosnia as part of the peacekeeping mission. During a briefing on land mines, the captain asks the soldiers if they have any questions.

Our intrepid solder raises his hand and asks, "If we do happen to step on a mine, sir, what do we do?"

"Normal procedure, Lieutenant, is to jump 200 feet in the air and scatter oneself over a wide area."

Brave Captain

Once upon a time, there was an officer of the Royal Canadian Navy named Captain Bravado who showed no fear when facing his enemies. One day, while sailing the Seven Seas, his lookout spots a pirate ship approaching, and the crew becomes frantic.

Captain Bravado bellows, "Bring me my red shirt!"

The first mate quickly retrieves the captain's red shirt, and while wearing the brightly coloured frock, the captain leads his crew into battle and defeats the mighty pirates. That evening, all the men sit around on deck recounting the triumph. One of them asks the captain, "Sir, why did you call for your red shirt before battle?"

The captain replies, "If I were to be wounded in the attack, the shirt would not show my blood. Thus, you men would continue to fight, unafraid."

All of the men marvelled at the courage of their captain.

At dawn the next morning, the lookout spots not one, not two, but 10 pirate ships approaching. The crew stares in worshipful silence at the captain and waits for his usual orders.

Captain Bravado gazes with steely eyes upon the vast armada heading for his ship, and without fear, turns and calmly shouts, "Get me my brown pants!"

At Peace

An office manager hires a new secretary. She is young, sweet, polite and just happens to be a former soldier in the Canadian Armed Forces.

One day while taking dictation, she notices the manager's fly is open. While leaving the room, she courteously says, "Oh, sir, did you know that your barracks door is open?"

Q: Why did the Canadian Navy switch to liquid soap?
A: It's harder to pick up.

The manager does not understand her remark, but later on he looks down and sees that his zipper is open. He decides to have some fun with his new employee. Calling her in, he says, "By the way, Miss Jones, when you saw my barracks door open this morning, did you also see a soldier standing at attention?"

The secretary replies, "No, sir. All I saw was a little disabled veteran sitting on two duffel bags."

AWOL

A Canadian soldier runs up to a nun on the street, and out of breath, he asks, "Please, may I hide under your skirt? I'll explain later." The nun agrees.

A moment later, two military police run up to the nun and ask, "Sister, have you seen a soldier?"

The nun replies, "He went that way," as she points down the road.

After the MPs run off, the soldier crawls out from under the skirt and says, "I can't thank you enough, sister. You see, I don't want to go to Afghanistan."

The nun says she understands completely.

The soldier adds, "I hope I'm not rude, but you have a great pair of legs."

The nun replies, "If you had looked a little higher, you would have also seen a great pair of balls. I don't want to go to Afghanistan either."

How to End the War in Afghanistan

The Department of Defence announced today the formation of a new 500-man elite fighting unit called the Canadian Hoser Elite Force

These good Canadian boys will be dropped into Afghanistan and will be given the following facts about terrorists:

1. The season opened today.
2. There is no limit on how many to kill.
3. They hate and mock hockey as a girl's sport.
4. They don't like beer, and they pray to Gary Bettman.
5. They are directly responsible for the NHL lockout.

The mess in Afghanistan should be over in a week.

Reinforcements

A big earthquake with the strength of 8.1 on the Richter scale has hit Mexico.

One hundred and fifty thousand Mexicans have died and over a million are injured. The country is totally ruined, and the government doesn't know where to start with providing help to rebuild. The rest of the world is in shock.

Canada is sending troopers to help the Mexican army control the rioting.

The European community (except France) is sending food and money.

The United States, not to be outdone, is sending 150,000 replacement Mexicans.

Bravery Tests

The top brass from the Canadian Armed Forces, the Canadian Navy and Special Forces are arguing about who has the bravest troops. They decide to settle the dispute using an enlisted man from each branch.

The army general calls a private over and orders him to climb to the top of the base flagpole while singing "The Caissons Go Rolling Along." He then has to let go with both hands and salute. The private quickly complies.

Next, the admiral orders a sailor to climb the pole, polish the brass knob at the top, sing "Anchors Aweigh," salute smartly and jump off. The sailor does as he is told and lands on the concrete below.

Finally, the Special Forces guy is told to do exactly as the army and navy men have done, but in full battle gear, pack filled with bricks, loaded weapon carried high.

He takes one look at the Special Forces general and says, "You're out of your mind, sir!"

The Special Forces commander turns to the others and says, "Now *that's* guts!"

Star Gazing

A Company Commander and the First Sergeant are in the field. As they hit the sack for the night, the sergeant says, "Sir, look up into the sky and tell me what you see."

The commander replies, "I see millions of stars."

Sergeant: "And what does that tell you, sir?"

Commander: "Astronomically, it tells me that there are millions of galaxies and potentially billions of planets. Theologically, it tells me that God is great, and that we are small and insignificant. Meteorologically, it tells me that we will have a beautiful day tomorrow. What does it tell you?"

Sergeant: "Well, sir, it tells me that somebody stole our tent."

Canadian Parachuting

As a sergeant in a parachute regiment, I took part in several night-time drills. Once, I sat next to a lieutenant fresh from jump school. He was quiet, sad and looked a bit pale, so I struck up a conversation.

"Scared, Lieutenant?" I asked.

He replied, "No, just a bit apprehensive."

I asked, "What's the difference?"

He replied, "That means I'm scared with a university education."

New Glasses

An army private goes to see the medical captain for a new pair of glasses. The captain looks in his book of records and says, "But you just got a new pair last month!"

"Yes sir, b...b...but I got them b...broken in an accident," stammers the private.

"Accident! What kind of an accident?"

The captain looks in his book of accident definitions and glossaries and says, "Road-march accident, Firing Range accident, PT accident, Drill accident?"

"N...no, n...no, none of those," says the private.

"Well, then, what is it?"

"I'd rather not tell you, sir..."

"Well, no satisfactory explanations, no new glasses," says the medical officer, ready to stand up. "I've got to see my other patients now."

"N...no, no, sir, wait! I broke them when I was kissing my girl," blurts the private.

"Don't be daft, man! How could you break your glasses kissing a girl?"

"Well...you see, she crossed her legs..."

Music Man

A Canadian solider stationed in Brazil writes to his wife, asking her to please send him a harmonica to occupy his free time and keep his mind off the local women.

The wife complies and sends the best harmonica she can find, along with several dozen lesson and music books.

Rotated back home months later, the soldier rushes to his home and runs through the front door. "Oh darling," he gushes, "come here...let me look at you...let me hold you! Let's have a fine dinner out, then make love all night. I've missed your lovin' so much!"

The wife, keeping her distance, says, "All in good time, lover. First, let's hear you play that harmonica."

❧ CHAPTER NINE ❧
A Canadian at School

Amazing Invention

In a grade four class at an Ottawa school, Miss Thurman asks her students to name the most important invention in the history of the world. A little girl puts up her hand.

"Yes, Courtney?" Miss Thurman says.

"The plane, Miss Thurman," she replies. "Now people can travel around the world really fast."

Another hand shoots up.

"Yes, Timmy?" Miss Thurman says.

"The telephone, because it was invented by a Canadian, and it helped people all over the world talk to each other."

"Very good, Timmy," replies the teacher.

"Miss Thurman, I know, I know!"

The teacher turns to see a little boy in the back row waving his arms back and forth like his life depended on it.

"Yes, Johnny. Go ahead."

"It's a thermos, Miss Thurman. It keeps hot things hot, and cold things cold, and no one has to tell it what to do!"

The Innocence of Children

In a suburban Vancouver school, a teacher is giving a class of grade one students a spelling lesson. He writes "cat" on the blackboard and says, "Now, Stella, what does that word mean?"

Little Stella stands up and answers correctly.

The teacher writes other words on the blackboard, and the students all promptly answer until the teacher writes the word "onion."

"Now you, Timmy," he says. "What does this word mean?"

Little Timmy stutters, flounders and at last confesses that he doesn't know the answer.

The teacher, trying to be as helpful as he can, says, "Why, Timmy, do you know what it is that your older sister always refuses to eat when she knows she'll be going out with her boyfriend later?"

"Oh sure!" Timmy screams. "Beans!"

The teacher continues the lesson after the laughter subsides and decides to move on to grammar. He writes the word "pencil" on the blackboard.

"Norma Jensen," says the teacher, "of what gender is that word?"

"It's a neutral gender, teacher," responds the proud little student.

"You are correct, little one," replies the teacher as he erases the word and writes down another. "Now you, Kathy, of what gender is the word 'man'?"

"Man is masculine gender, teacher," Kathy says with pride.

"That's right," says the teacher, who again erases the word and writes down another. "And now you again, Timmy. What gender is 'cat'?"

"Hmmm," replies the little boy. "You have to show me the cat first."

History Lesson

Mom: "Why aren't you doing well in school, Johnny? Look, you got a 'D' in Canadian history!"

Johnny: "It's not my fault! The teacher keeps asking about things that happened before I was born."

Beauty Lesson

In a Canadian history discussion group, a professor is trying to explain how society's ideal of beauty changes with time. "For example," she says, "take the 1921 Miss Canada. She stood five feet, one inch tall, weighed 108 pounds and had measurements of 30-25-32. How do you think she'd do in today's version of the pageant?"

The class falls silent for a moment. Then one student pipes up, "Not very well."

"Why is that?" asks the professor.

"For one thing," the student points out, "she'd be about 100 years old."

University Discussion

Three aspiring psychiatrists from different universities in Canada attend their first class on emotional extremes.

"Just to establish some parameters," says the professor to the University of Toronto student, "what is the opposite of joy?"

"Sadness," responds the student.

"And the opposite of depression?" he asks the student from McGill.

"Elation," is her reply.

"And you, sir," he says to the young man from the University of Alberta. "What is the opposite of woe?"

The student says, "Sir, that would be giddy up."

Homework

There is a university in New Brunswick where the students operate a "bank" of term papers and other homework assignments. There are papers to suit all needs and subjects. Since it would look odd if an undistinguished student suddenly handed in a brilliant essay, there are papers for an A grade, B grade and C grade.

Shortest Canadian Book: *Career Options for Arts Grads*

One student, who has spent the weekend on more "extra-curricular pursuits," goes to the bank, and as his course was a standard one, he takes out a paper for an inconspicuous C. He then retypes it and hands the work in.

In due course, the student receives the paper back with the professor's comments: "I wrote this paper myself 20 years ago. I always thought it was worth an A, and now I'm pleased to give it one!"

Snowing on Campus

It has been snowing for hours at McGill University when an announcement comes over the intercom: "Will the students who are parked on University Drive please move their cars so that we may begin plowing." Twenty minutes later, there is another announcement: "Will the 900 students who went to move 14 cars please return to class."

Summer Vacation

Little Johnny's class has returned to school from their summer vacation. The teacher asks all the students in the class to go up to the chalkboard and draw a picture to describe their summer.

The first to go is Sarah. She draws a sailboat and says, "This summer me and my family rented a boat and sailed all around Newfoundland."

The teacher says, "That's very nice, Sarah."

Q: How many Lakehead students does it take to change a light bulb?

A: None. Thunder Bay doesn't have electricity, remember?

Next, Julie goes up to the board and draws a sandy beach and a big sun. Julie says, "My family and I went to the beach for the summer."

The teacher says, "That must have been fun."

Next, it is Little Johnny's turn. He walks up to the chalkboard and draws a dot on the board.

The teacher says, "What is that, Johnny? Is it a dot or a ball or what?"

Little Johnny replies, "No, that's a period. My sister missed hers this summer, and that's why we didn't have a summer vacation."

Language Lesson

Three French students learning English at the University of Calgary are discussing the professor's wife who has been married to the professor for many years and is still childless.

"She's barren," the first student says.

"No, no, that's not the correct word," the second student volunteers. "The correct word is 'infertile.'"

The third student says, "You're both wrong; the correct word is 'impregnable.'"

Dorm Rules

On the first day of classes at Dalhousie University, a professor points out some of the school's rules to the students:

"The female dormitory will be out-of-bounds to all male students, and the male dormitory to the female students. Anybody caught breaking this rule will be fined $25 the first time. Anybody caught breaking this rule a second time will be fined $75. Being caught a third time will cost you $225. Are there any questions?"

At this point, a male student in the crowd inquires, "How much for a season's pass?"

Top 10 Reasons that University Is Like Preschool

10. You cry for your mother.
9. You cross the street without looking for cars.
8. Snack time is a necessity.
7. You bundle up for the outdoors without caring what you look like because everyone else looks as stupid as you do.
6. You stay at home and play games with your friends.
5. You wear your backpack on both shoulders.
4. You wear big mittens.
3. Playing in the snow is a legitimate activity.
2. You take naps
1. You look forward to grilled cheese sandwiches and Kraft Dinner.

Schooled

A friendly baseball game recently took place in Montréal between a group of McGill University students and a team made up of teaching assistants and professors. Before the game, the two designated captains meet on the field to exchange pleasantries.

The two shake hands, and the student leader says, "May the best team win!"

The university captain, a professor of English, replies, "You mean, may the *better* team win!"

Lesson from Dad

A math teacher asks one of his students if he knows his numbers.

"Yes," Johnny replies. "I do. My dad taught me."

"Good. What comes after three?"

"Four," answers the boy.

"What comes after six?"

"Seven."

"That's correct," says the teacher. "Your father did a good job. What comes after 10?"

"A Canadian Club," says Johnny.

Signs that You've Been in University Too Long

- You actually like doing laundry at home.

- Two kilometres is not too far to walk for a party.

- You'd rather clean than study.

- "Oh crap, how did it get so late!" comes out of your mouth at least once a night.

- Mom's meatloaf and potatoes become something you desire, not avoid.

- You schedule your classes around sleep habits and the TV show *Big Bang Theory.*

- You and the pizza boy are on a first-name basis.

- You go to sleep when it's light and get up when it's dark.

- You live for getting mail.

- Gazing out the window is a form of entertainment.

- Prank phone calls become funny again.

- You start thinking and sounding like your roommate.

- Black lights and highlighters are the coolest things on earth.

- Rearranging your room is your favourite pastime.

- You think Walmart is the coolest store.

- The weekend lasts from Thursday to Sunday.

Project

A group of young students return to class Monday morning in their upper-class neighbourhood in Toronto. They are very excited. Their weekend assignment was to sell something, then give a talk to the class on productive salesmanship.

Little Sally leads off. "I sold Girl Guide cookies, and I made $30," she says proudly. "My sales approach was to appeal to the customer's civil spirit, and I credit that approach for my obvious success."

"Very good," says the teacher.

Little Jenny was next. "I sold magazines," she says. "I made $45, and I explained to everyone that magazines would keep them up on current events."

"Very good, Jenny," replies the teacher.

Eventually, it is Little Johnny's turn.

Little Johnny walks to the front of the classroom and dumps a box full of cash on the teacher's desk.

"I made $2467," he says.

"$2467!" cries the teacher. "What in the world were you selling?"

"Toothbrushes," replies Little Johnny.

"Toothbrushes?" echoes the teacher. "How could you possibly sell enough toothbrushes to make that much money?"

"I found the busiest corner in town," says Little Johnny, "and I set up a chip-and-dip stand, and then I gave everybody who walked by a sample. They all said the same thing: 'Hey, this tastes like shit!' Then I would say, 'It is shit. Wanna buy a toothbrush?'"

Proper Manners

During a grade six class in Sudbury, a teacher is explaining good manners to her students. She says, "Students, if you were on a date and having supper with a nice young lady, how would you tell her that you have to go to the bathroom? Michael?"

Michael: "I'd say, 'Just a minute, I have to go pee.'"

Teacher: "That would be rude and impolite. What about you, Peter? How would you say it?"

Peter: "I'd say, 'I'm sorry, but I really need to go to the bathroom. I'll be right back.'"

Teacher: "That's better, but it's still not very nice to say the word 'bathroom' at the dinner table. And you, Johnny? Are you able to use your intelligence for once and show us your good manners?"

Johnny: "I would say, 'Darling, may I please be excused for a moment? I have to shake hands with a very dear friend of mine who I hope you'll get to meet after supper.'"

The teacher faints.

Motivation

A mother and father are worried about their son Paul who refuses to learn math at school, so they send him to a Montréal Catholic school that has a good reputation for teaching the subject. After his first day at the school, Paul comes home, runs straight to his room and slams the door. This behaviour continues every school night for the next two months, at which time the school contacts the parents and asks them to meet with their son's math teacher.

Paul's parents fear the worst, but to their surprise, the math teacher reveals that Paul is doing excellent work and is at the top of his class.

The parents leave the meeting feeling relieved, and when they get home, they ask their son, "So what changed your mind about learning math?"

"Well," says Paul, "on the first day I walked into the classroom, I saw a guy nailed to a plus sign at the back of the room, and I knew they meant business."

Assignment

Grade three students in a Catholic school in Regina are asked to write a story with a moral. The next day, they read out their stories to the teacher.

The first up is Valerie. "My daddy owns a farm, and every Sunday we put the chicken eggs on the truck and drive to town to sell them at market. But one Sunday, we hit a bump on the road, and all the eggs fell on the ground and smashed. And the moral of the story is: don't put all your eggs in one basket."

"Very nice, Valerie," says the teacher. "Now you, Jane."

Jane reads her story. "My daddy also owns a farm. Every weekend we take the chickens eggs and put them in an incubator. Last weekend, only 8 of the 12 eggs hatched. And the moral of the story is: don't count your chickens before they hatch."

"Very nice, Jane," says the teacher. "Now, let's hear from you, Jonathan."

"My grandfather fought in World War II, and one day his plane was shot down," says Jonathan. "He parachuted out before the plane crashed, and he managed to grab a case of beer, a machine gun and a machete. He drank the case of beer on the way down and landed in the middle of 1000 enemy soldiers. He killed 500 Germans with his machine gun, and when he ran out of bullets, he killed another 125 with his machete and throttled 25 more with his bare hands before the enemy retreated."

"That's a very colourful story, Jonathan," says the teacher, "but what is the moral of the story?"

"Don't mess with my grandfather when he's drunk."

Marketing Concepts

A professor at the University of British Columbia is explaining marketing concepts to his students using different examples.

1. "You see a gorgeous girl at a party. You go up to her and say, 'I'm very rich. Marry me!' That's Direct Marketing."

2. "You're at a party with a bunch of friends and see a gorgeous girl. One of your friends goes up to her and, pointing at you, says, 'He's very rich. Marry him.' That's Advertising."

3. "You see a gorgeous girl at a party. You go up to her and get her telephone number. The next day, you call and say, 'Hi. I'm very rich. Marry me.' That's Telemarketing."

4. "You're at a party and see gorgeous girl. You get up, straighten your tie, walk up to her and offer her a drink. Later on, you open the car door for her when you drive her home then say, 'By the way, I'm rich. Will you marry me?' That's Public Relations."

5. "You're at a party and see gorgeous girl. She walks up to you and says, 'You are very rich! Will you marry me?' That's Brand Recognition."

6. "You see a gorgeous girl at a party. You go up to her and say, 'I'm very rich. Marry me!' She slaps your face. That's Customer Feedback."

7. "You see a gorgeous girl at a party. You go up to her and say, 'I'm very rich. Marry me!' And she introduces you to her husband. That's Demand and Supply Gap."

8. "You see a gorgeous girl at a party. You go up to her, and before you say anything, another man comes up to her and says, 'I'm rich. Will you marry me?' And she leaves the party with him. That's Competition Eating into your Market Share."

9. "You see a gorgeous girl at a party. You go up to her, and before you say, 'I'm rich, Marry me!' your wife arrives. That's Restriction for Entering New Markets."

Underemployed

A University of Alberta student has a part-time job delivering pizza and arrives at the home of Larry, who lives in a trailer on the outskirts of Edmonton. After the student hands over the pizza, Larry asks, "What is the usual tip?"

"Well," replies the student, "this is my first trip here, but the other guys say if I get a quarter out of you, I'll be doing great."

"Is that so?" snorts Larry. "Well, just to show them how wrong they are, here's five dollars."

"Thanks," replies the student. "I'll put this in my school fund."

"What are you studying?" asks Larry.

The student pockets the five dollars, smiles and says, "Applied psychology."

Putting Up with Jocks

The coach for the McGill University football team storms into the president's office and demands a raise right then and there.

"Please," protests the college president, "you already make more than the entire history department."

"Yeah, maybe so, but you don't know what I have to put up with," the coach complains. "Watch." The coach walks out into the hall and grabs the first jock he sees and says to him, "Run over to my office and see if I'm there."

Twenty minutes later, the jock returns, sweaty and out of breath.

"You're not there, sir," the jock reports.

"Oh, I see what you mean," says the president, scratching his head. "I would have phoned."

CHAPTER TEN

A Canadian Family

Kid Questions

In a rural Québec home, a young girl asks her mother a question.

"Maman, where did I come from?"

"Why, ma cheri, what a funny question for you to ask!" replies the mother. "The stork brought you to me in a nice big basket, of course."

"And where did you come from, Maman?" asks the little girl.

"Why," says the mother, "the stork brought me to your dear old grandmamma in a basket just the same way, darling."

"Then where did granny come from," she asks again.

"Oh, your grandmamma was brought by the same stork in exactly the same manner," replies the mother.

"Maman!" screams the little girl. "Are you telling me there hasn't been a real man in this family for three generations?"

Family Diary

August 12

We moved to our new home in Winnipeg. It's so beautiful here. The prairies are so vast, and I can hardly wait to see the fields covered with snow. Love it here.

October 14

Winnipeg is the most beautiful place on earth. All the leaves have turned different shades of red and orange. Went for a ride through the beautiful farmland and saw some deer. They are so graceful and certainly the most beautiful creature on earth. This must be paradise. I love it here.

November 11

Deer hunting season starts soon. I can't imagine anyone wanting to kill such a beautiful creature. Hope it will snow soon.

December 2

It snowed last night. Woke up to find everything blanketed in white. It looks like a postcard. I went outside and cleaned the snow off the steps and shovelled the driveway. We built a snowman. What a beautiful place. I love Winnipeg. When the snowplow came by, I had to shovel the driveway again.

December 12

More snow last night. Couldn't get out of the driveway to get to work. I'm exhausted shovelling snow. Friggen snowplow!

December 22

More of that white shit fell last night. I've got blisters on my hands from shovelling. I think that snowplow hides around the corner and waits until I'm done shovelling the driveway. Asshole!

December 25

Merry effin' Christmas! More friggen snow. If I ever get my hands on that son of a bitch who drives that snowplow, I swear I'll kill the bastard. Don't know why they don't use more salt on the roads to melt the friggen snow.

December 28

More white shit last night. Been inside for three days, except for shovelling out the driveway every time the snowplow goes by. Can't go anywhere; car's stuck in a mountain of white shit. The weatherman says to expect another 10 inches again tonight!

December 29

The damn weatherman was wrong. We got 24 inches of that white shit this time! At this rate it won't melt before next summer. The snowplow got stuck up the road, and that bastard came to the door and asked to borrow my shovel. After I told him how I had broken six shovels already from shovelling all the shit he pushed into my driveway, I broke my last shovel over his head.

January 3

Finally got out of the house today. Drove to the store to get food and on my way back, a deer ran out in front of the car, and I hit it. Did about $3000 damage to the car. Those effin' beasts should be killed. Wish the hunters had killed them all last November!

May 3

Moved to Vancouver. I can't imagine why anyone in their right mind would ever live in the God-forsaken province of Manitoba.

Letter to Dad

In a quiet Windsor neighbourhood, a father walks by his son's bedroom and is astonished to see the bed nicely made and everything picked up. Then he sees an envelope propped up prominently at the centre of the bed. It is addressed "Dad." Fearing the worst, he opens the envelope and reads the letter with trembling hands:

Dear Dad,

It is with great regret and sorrow that I'm writing you. I had to elope with my new girlfriend because I wanted to avoid a scene with you and Mom. I've found real passion with Joan, and she is so nice, even with all her piercings, tattoos and Harley-Davidson clothes.

Oh, and one other thing, Dad. Joan is pregnant, and she says we'll be very happy. Even though you might not care for her because she is much older than me, she already owns a trailer in the woods and has a big stack of firewood for the whole winter. She wants to have many more children with me, and that's now one of my dreams too.

Joan taught me that marijuana doesn't really hurt anyone, and we'll be growing it for us and trading it with her friends for all the cocaine and ecstasy we want. In the meantime, we'll pray that science will find a cure for AIDS so Joan can get better; she sure deserves it!

Don't worry, Dad, I'm 15 years old now, and I know how to take care of myself. Someday I'm sure we'll be back to visit so you can get to know your grandchildren.

Your son, John

PS: Dad, none of the above is true. I'm over at the neighbour's house. I just wanted to remind you that there are worse things in life than my report card that's in my desk drawer. I love you! Text me when it's safe for me to come home.

Final Wishes

Paul from Ottawa is getting his affairs in order. He has his lawyer prepare his will and then makes his final arrangements.

Paul meets with his priest to discuss the type of funeral service he wants. He also tells the priest he wants to be cremated, and he wants his ashes scattered over a Tim Hortons.

"Tim Hortons!" cries the priest. "Why Timmy's?"

"So that my sons will visit me every day."

Visiting

Mike is visiting his 90-year-old grandfather in an isolated area of northern Ontario.

After the spending the night, Mike wakes up to find his grandfather cooking a breakfast of eggs and bacon. Mike notices a filmy substance on his plate, and he says to his grandfather, "Are these plates clean?"

His grandfather replies, "Those plates are as clean as cold water can get them, so go on and finish your breakfast."

Q: How do you know if you're a hoser?

A: You think the phrase "loading the dishwasher" means getting your old lady drunk.

That afternoon, while eating the hamburgers his grandfather makes for lunch, Mike notices tiny specks around the edge of his plate and a substance that looks like dried egg yokes, so he asks again, "Are you sure these plates are clean?"

Without looking up from his hamburger, the grandfather says, "I told you before; those dishes are as clean as cold water can get them. Now, don't ask me about it anymore!"

Later that afternoon, Mike is on his way out to get dinner in a nearby town. As he is leaving, his grandfather's dog starts to growl and doesn't let him pass so he says, "Grandpa, your dog won't let me out."

Without diverting his attention from the hockey game he is watching on TV, the grandfather shouts, "Cold Water, go lay down!"

New Neighbours

A snobbish professional couple moves to a new neighbourhood in Toronto, and next door from them is a couple from Jamaica with four kids.

One day, while the two mothers are watching their children playing in their backyards, the snobbish mother turns to the Jamaican woman and says, "You know, it's amazing…I've got three kids, and they all turned out white and ugly as hell, but you have four kids and every one of them came out black and cute as hell. What's your secret?"

The Jamaican woman is mystified by the stupid question, so she decides to string her neighbour along. "Well," she says, "it all depends on the size of your husband's penis."

"How so?"

"Is your husband's dick at least 10 inches long?" asks the Jamaican lady.

"Oh, no! Not nearly that big," the woman replies.

"All right, that's okay," says the Jamaican mom. "But is it at least two inches thick?"

"Heavens to Betsy, no!" she replies.

"Well, then, there's your problem, sister," says the Jamaican mom. "You're letting in too much light."

Family Dynamics

An elderly man in Victoria calls his son Bob in Toronto and says, "I hate to ruin your day, son, but your mother and I are divorcing. Forty-five years of misery is enough! I'm sick of her, and I'm sick of talking about this, so call your sister in Montréal and tell her." He hangs up.

The son frantically calls his sister, who goes nuts upon hearing the news.

She calls her father and yells, "You are *not* getting a divorce! Bob and I will be there tomorrow. Until then, don't do a single thing! Do you hear me?"

The father hangs up the phone, turns to his wife and says, "It worked! The kids are coming for a visit, and they're paying their own way!"

Big Family

An Québec woman is at the welfare office filling out forms. The clerk asks her how many children she has.

"Ten boys."

"And what are their names?"

"Pierre, Pierre, Pierre, Pierre, Pierre, Pierre, Pierre, Pierre, Pierre and the youngest is Pierre."

"All your sons are named 'Pierre'? Why would you name them all 'Pierre'?"

"Dat way, when I wants dem all to come in from the yard, I just yells, 'Pierre!' And when I want dem all to come inside for dinner, I just yells, 'Pierre!'"

"What if you just want a particular son to do something?"

"Den I call him by his last name."

Canadian Logic

An 80-year-old man is having his annual medical check-up.

The doctor asks him how he is doing.

"I've never been better!" the old man replies. "I have a 20-year-old bride who is pregnant with my child! What do you think about that?"

The doctor considers this for a moment and then says, "Well, let me tell you a story.... I know a guy who is an avid hunter. He never misses a hunting season. But one day, he is in a bit of a hurry, and he accidentally grabs his umbrella instead of his gun. He walks into the woods near a creek and spots a deer in some brush in front of him. He raises his umbrella, points it at the deer and squeezes the handle. And BAM, the deer drops dead in front of him."

"That's impossible!" says the old man in disbelief. "Someone else must have shot that deer!"

"Exactly," says the doctor.

Pet Protector

Harold's new job has him working really late. He decides to get his wife a watchdog because they live in a dangerous part of Saskatoon. He goes to the pet store and asks for a Doberman.

The employee says, "If it's a guard dog you want, sir, I have just the dog for you." The girl walks to the back of the store and returns carrying a little poodle.

Harold says, "This small thing is a watch dog? You're kidding, right?"

The young woman says, "No, this dog is special. He knows karate."

"Karate? I don't believe it," says Harold.

The employee puts the small dog down on the floor, points to a sign advertising dog food and says, "Karate the sign!" The dog runs up to the sign and rips it to shreds.

Harold is amazed at this.

The employee then points to a chair and says, "Karate the chair!" The dog runs up to the chair and rips it to shreds.

By now Harold is convinced. "I'll take him," he says.

When Harold gets home, he surprises his wife with the poodle.

She yells out, "This little thing is a watch dog? Ha! No way!"

Harold says, "But this dog knows karate!"

"Karate? Ha!" she yells. "Karate my ass!"

Cheating Heart

A man in Halifax is having an affair with a married woman. While she and her lover are in her bedroom one afternoon, her husband comes home early from work. The woman jumps up and tells her lover to go into the bathroom to hide. Just as she is hiding his clothes under the bed, the husband opens the bedroom door and walks in.

He asks, "What the hell are you doing?"

Thinking quickly, the wife says, "Umm...I'm waiting for you."

The suspicious husband looks at her in disbelief and says, "But you're naked."

Again the woman says, "Yeah...I was waiting for you."

The husband relaxes and says, "Hold on! I'm going to jump in the shower. I'll be back in a flash!"

The wife tries to stop him, but he just ignores her and rushes for the bathroom. When the husband opens the bathroom door, he sees a naked man jumping around and clapping.

The husband asks, "What in the hell are you doing in here?"

The man replies, "I'm the exterminator, and your wife called saying you guys had a problem with moths. With the dampness, they are a real problem, eh."

The husband looks him over and says, "But you're naked."

The man looks down, jumps in surprise and mutters, "Them little bastards!"

Door to Door

On a quiet Sunday morning in Regina, a middle-aged woman answers the door to a market researcher.

"Good morning, madam. I'm doing some market research for Vaseline. Do you use this product in your household?"

"Oh yes, all the time. It's very good on cuts and burns."

"Do you use it for anything else?"

"Like what?" asks the woman.

"Ahem...err...well...during...ahem...sex?"

"Oh, yes, of course. I smear it on the bedroom doorknob to keep my husband out!"

Date Night

A couple in Ottawa is ready to go out for a night on the town and call a taxi. When the taxi arrives, the husband shuts off the lights, grabs the house keys and puts the cat out.

As the husband is ready to shut the front door, the cat shoots back into the house. They don't want the cat shut in the house, so the wife walks out to the taxi while the husband goes upstairs to chase the cat out.

The wife, not wanting it known that the house will be empty while they are away, explains to the taxi driver, "He's just going upstairs to say goodbye to my mother."

A few minutes later, the husband gets into the taxi. "Sorry I took so long," he says. "Stupid old thing was hiding under the bed, and I had to poke her with a coat hanger to get her to come out!"

Young Love

A young couple from Calgary are deeply in love and plan to marry, but on the night before their wedding, they are involved in a serious car accident, and both are killed. Now in heaven, the couple approaches St. Peter.

"My fiancée and I are really disappointed that we couldn't celebrate our wedding vows," says the young man. "Is it possible for people in heaven to get married?"

St. Peter replies, "I'll tell you what—after you have gone through an appropriate waiting period, we will talk about it again."

Five years pass, and the couple still wants to get married. They approach St. Peter again and ask him if enough time has passed so that they can get married.

"I'm sorry," replies St. Peter. "I know five years is a long time to wait when you're in love, but there's been a slight problem. You'll have to wait a little bit longer."

Another five years pass, and St. Peter approaches the couple one day. "Your wait is over!" he says. "You may now marry. Thank you for your patience."

The couple is overjoyed and gets married.

Unfortunately, soon after the wedding, the couple realizes they are not compatible. They go to see St. Peter once more and ask him if there is such a thing as divorce in heaven.

St. Peter gives them a cold stare and says sternly, "Look, it took us 10 years to find a minister up here. Do you have any idea how long it'll take to find a lawyer?"

For Rent

A couple with seven children moves to Toronto. They are having a difficult time finding an apartment to live in. Many of the apartments they look at are large enough, but the landlords refuse to rent to such a large family.

The family stays in a motel, and after several days of searching for a place to live, the husband asks his wife to take the four younger children to visit the nearby cemetery, while he takes the older three with him to find an apartment. After the father and the three kids spend most of the morning searching for an apartment, they find a place that is just right.

Then the landlord asks the father the usual question, "How many children do you have?"

"Seven," the father says with a deep sigh. "But four are with their dear mother in the cemetery."

The landlord, feeling sympathetic toward the man's situation, rents the apartment to him.

Fear of Flying

Old Aunt Bessie lives in Prince Edward Island and loves to visit her nieces and nephews. However, she has relatives all across Canada, and the problem is that no matter how much she enjoys seeing her family, she hates flying. Everyone tells her that flying is safe, but she always worries that someone will have a bomb on the plane.

She reads books about how safe flying is and even gets a flight attendant to demonstrate all the safety features on airplanes. But Aunt Bessie still worries herself silly every time her family asks her to fly out to visit them.

Finally, the family decides that maybe if Aunt Bessie sees the statistics, she'd be convinced that flying is a safe form of travel. So they send her to a friend of the family who is an actuary.

"Tell me," she asks the actuary, "what are the chances that someone will have a bomb on a plane?"

The actuary looks through the tables and statistics and finally says, "A very small chance. Maybe one in 500,000."

Aunt Bessie nods, then thinks for a moment. She says, "So what are the odds of *two* people having a bomb on the same plane?"

Again the man studies the stats and says, "Extremely remote. About one in a billion."

Aunt Bessie nods, thanks the man for his time and leaves his office.

And from that day forward, every time she flies, Aunt Bessie takes a bomb with her.

Family Discord

Jenny's husband, Charlie, is a typical Canadian male chauvinist. Even though they both work full time, Charlie never helps with the chores around the house. He thinks housework is woman's work. But one evening, Jenny arrives home from work to find the children bathed, one load of clothes in the washer and another in the dryer, dinner on the stove and the table set. She is astonished!

Q: How many honest and caring men in the world does it take to do the dishes?

A: Both of them.

"Something must be up," she thinks to herself.

It turns out that Charlie read an article that said wives who worked full time and had to do all the housework were too tired to have sex.

The next day, Jennie tells her friends at work all about her night.

"We had a great dinner. Charlie even did the dishes! And he also helped the kids with their homework, folded all the laundry and put everything away. I really enjoyed the evening."

"But what about afterward?" asks one of her friends.

"Oh, that was perfect too," replies Jennie. "Charlie was too tired!"

Doctor's Advice

A doctor is lecturing a large audience in Vancouver about living a healthy lifestyle. "The material we put into our stomachs is enough to have killed most of us sitting here years ago," says the doctor. "Red meat is awful. Soft drinks corrode the stomach lining. Chinese food is loaded with MSG. High-fat diets are disastrous to our health, and none of us realizes the long-term harm caused by the bacteria in our drinking water. But there is one thing that is the most dangerous material of all, and we have all eaten it—or will eat it. Can anyone tell me what food it is that causes the most damage and suffering for years after eating it?"

After several seconds of silence, a 75-year-old man in the front row raises his hand and softly says, "Wedding cake."

Book Club

Melvin and Joe are sitting in Starbucks having a coffee.

"My wife suggested a book for me to read to enhance our relationship," says Melvin. "It's called *Women Are from Venus, Men Are Wrong.*"

Divorce Talk

Bill and Earl are in Banff sitting in a boat on a lake fishing and sucking down some Molson Canadian when all of a sudden Bill says, "I think I'm going to divorce my wife. She hasn't spoken to me in over three months."

Earl grabs another beer then says, "You better think it over. Women like that are hard to find."

Four-letter Words

A young couple from Saskatoon gets married, and when they get back from their honeymoon, the new bride immediately phones her mother.

"Well," says her mother, "how was the honeymoon, darling?"

"Oh, Mama," the bride replies, "the honeymoon was wonderful! So romantic..." Then suddenly, she bursts out crying. "But, Mama, as soon as we returned, Sam started using the most horrible language. He said things I've never heard before! I mean...all these awful four-letter words! You've got to let me come home. Please, Mama!"

"Sarah, Sarah," her mother says. "Calm down! You need to stay with your husband and work this out. Now, tell me, what could be so awful? What four-letter words did he use?"

"Please don't make me tell you, Mama," cries the daughter. "I'm so embarrassed. They're just too awful! Come get me, please!"

"Darling, baby, you must tell me what has you so upset. Tell your mama what these horrible four-letter words were!"

Still sobbing, the bride says, "Oh, Mama! He used words like dust, wash, iron, cook..."

"I'll pick you up in 20 minutes," says the mother.

Suspicious Mom

A young girl from northern Ontario leaves home to find work in the bright lights of Toronto.

She returns home six months later for a visit and steps out of a taxi wearing a full-length mink coat.

"Wow, Colleen," says her mother. "That is a lovely soft coat you are wearing, and it looks so expensive. Where did ye get that?"

Colleen replies, "Sure now, I won it at the bingo. Don't they have wonderful prizes in Toronto?"

When the weekend is over, Colleen returns to Toronto, but she goes back home to visit her mom a few months later. This time, when she steps out of the taxi, she's wearing a beautiful gold wrist-watch and a large diamond ring.

The mom again asks her daughter where she got the beautiful gifts, and Colleen again says, "I won it at bingo!"

Colleen returns to the bright lights again. A few months later, she returns home sporting an expensive emerald-and-diamond necklace with matching bracelet and earrings. She hands her mother $1000 and explains that she won it all at bingo.

Then Colleen asks her mom to run her a bath because she would like to freshen up.

When Colleen goes into the bathroom, she notices that there is only an inch of water in the bathtub. Colleen, a bit peeved at her mom being so cheap with the hot water after being handed $1000, calls downstairs, "Mom! Didn't I ask you to run me a bath? There's only an inch of water in the tub!"

"Indeed there is, darling," replies the mom. "But we don't want your bingo card getting wet now, do we?"

Moral of the story: You can never fool your mom.

Faded Love

A Polish man moves to Canada and marries a Canadian girl. Although his English is far from perfect, the couple gets along very well. One day the husband rushes into a lawyer's office and asks him if he can arrange a divorce for him. The lawyer tells the man that getting a divorce will depend on the circumstances. The lawyer asks the husband a few questions.

"Why do you want to get a divorce?"

"She going to kill me!"

"What makes you think that?"

"I got proof!"

"What kind of proof?"

"She going to poison me. She buy a bottle at drugstore and put on shelf in bathroom. I can read, and it say 'Polish Remover'!"

Smart Canadian Boy

A man in a Florida supermarket tries to buy half a head of lettuce.

The young produce assistant tells him that the store sells only whole heads of lettuce. The customer persists and asks to see the manager. The boy goes to find the manager.

Walking into the back room, the boy says to his manager, "Some asshole wants to buy half a head of lettuce."

Just as the boy is finishing his sentence, he turns to find the man standing right behind him, so he adds, "And this gentleman has kindly offered to buy the other half."

The manager approves the deal, and the man leaves the store happy.

Later, the manager says to the boy, "I was impressed with the way you got yourself out of that situation earlier. We like employees who think on their feet. Where are you from, son?"

"Canada, sir," the boy replies.

"Well, why did you leave Canada?" the manager asks.

The boy replies, "Sir, there's nothing but whores and hockey players up there."

"Really?" says the manager. "My wife is from Canada."

"No shit?" replies the boy. "Who'd she play for?"

Till the End

A funeral service is being held for a woman who has just passed away.

At the end of the service, the pallbearers are carrying the casket out when they accidentally bump into a wall, jarring the casket.

They hear a faint moan. They open the casket and find that the woman is actually alive! She lives for 10 more years and then finally dies.

The funeral is again held at the same place, and at the end of the ceremony, the pallbearers are again carrying out the casket. As they are walking, the husband cries out, "Watch out for the wall!"

Alberta Love

"Peter, I want you to get me a divorce," a burly man from Calgary tells his lawyer. "That wife of mine ain't behavin' right. She's *my* woman, and she's supposed to do what I say."

"Well, Mike, a wife isn't exactly property, you know," says Peter. "You don't own her the way you own an oil well."

"Maybe not," Mike replies, "but I damn well oughta have exclusive drilling rights."

CHAPTER ELEVEN

A Canadian Oot and Aboot

Roll It Up

A blonde woman in Edmonton orders a coffee at Tim Hortons and notices a "Roll Up the Rim to Win" sticker on her coffee cup. So she rolls up the rim on her coffee cup and starts screaming, "I've won a motorhome! I've won a motorhome!"

Everyone in the shop stares at the woman as she keeps on screaming, "I've won a motorhome! I've won a motorhome!"

Finally, the manager goes over to the woman and says, "Ma'am, I'm sorry, but you're mistaken. You couldn't have possibly won a motorhome because that's not one of the prizes!"

The woman says, "No, it's not a mistake. I've won a motorhome!"

She hands the cup to the manager, and he reads out loud "Win-a-Bagel."

Order Up

Man: "I'll have me a hot dog, a poutine and a Pepsi."

Guy behind the counter: "You must be from Québec."

Man: "What the hell kind of stereotypical remark is that? If I walked in here and asked for a sausage, would you think I was German?"

Guy: "No."

Man: "If I walked in here and asked for some pizza, would you think I was Italian?"

Guy: "No."

Man: "And if I walked in here and asked for some chow mein, would you presume I was Chinese?"

Guy: "No."

Man: "Then what makes you think I'm from Québec?"

Guy: "Well, because you are at the hardware store, sir."

Prison Sentence

Two boys from Toronto get busted for possession of drugs. When they go to court the next day, the judge reprimands them.

"I cannot believe the number of young people who appear in my court for use of illegal drugs," he says. "But because this is the first offence for both of you, I'm going to give you a break. If each of you can get 10 of your friends in your neighbourhood to sign a pledge vowing to give up illegal drugs for life, I'll let you off with a warning."

Without hesitating, the two kids agree to try to get the signatures.

A week later, they are back in court before the same judge. "How did you make out with your assignment? I hope you will not make me send you away," the judge says to the two boys.

The first kid stands up and says, "Your honour, I got 10 signatures."

"Good for you," says the judge. "And how did you get them to sign?"

"Well, I remembered this old anti-drug commercial, so I drew a dot and a circle on a piece of paper, then pointed to the dot and said, 'This is the size of your brain when you're on drugs.' Then I pointed at the circle and said, 'This is the size of your brain when you're not on drugs,' and they all signed the pledge," says the boy with pride.

"Very good job, young man," says the judge. "You are free to go."

Then the judge looks at the second kid and asks him how many signatures he was able to collect.

"One hundred and fifty," replies the boy.

"That's incredible!" says the judge. "How did you accomplish that?"

"Well, it was easy for me," says the kid. "I also drew a dot and a circle on a piece of paper. Then I pointed to the dot and said, 'This here dot is the size of your asshole before you go to prison...and this one is...'"

Boring Book

A Newfie storms up to the front desk of his local library and says, "I have a complaint!"

"Yes, sir?" says the librarian looking up at him.

"I borrowed a book from this library last week, and it was horrible!"

Puzzled by his complaint, the librarian asks, "What was wrong with the book?"

"It had way too many characters, and there was no plot whatsoever!" says the Newfie.

The librarian nods and says, "Ahhh. So you must be the person who took our phone book."

Sharpshooter

A man in a state of excessive inebriation rolls up to a fairground rifle range booth in Ponoka, Alberta, and throws down the necessary money. The booth operator at first refuses to let him take a turn, considering that his inebriated state could endanger the public. But the drunk insists, so the booth operator hands him a gun.

The drunk aims the rifle unsteadily in the general direction of the target, and after trying to focus, pulls the trigger three times. The booth owner, on inspecting the target, is astonished to see that the drunk man has scored three bulls-eyes. The star prize is a set of glassware, but the operator decides that the drunk isn't even aware of what he has done, so he gives him a consolation prize instead—a small, live turtle. The drunk wanders off into the crowd.

An hour or so later, the man comes back, even more drunk than before. Once again the booth operator demurs, but the drunk insists on playing, and once more he scores three bulls-eyes and is given another turtle.

Eventually the drunk rolls up again and insists on a third attempt. He picks up the rifle, waves it around in the general direction of the target and pulls the trigger three times. He again scores three bulls-eyes. But this time, an onlooker with good eyesight says, "That's fantastic. Hasn't he scored three bulls-eyes?"

The operator, cursing his luck, makes a show of going over to the target and inspecting it closely.

"Yes, sir!" he announces to the crowd. "This is fantastic! Congratulations, sir, you have won the star prize of a magnificent 68-piece set of glassware!"

"I don't want any bloody glasses," the drunk replies. "Give me another one of those little crusty meat pies!"

May I Take Your Order?

A guest in a Nova Scotia seaside hotel is sitting in a restaurant and calls over the head waiter one morning.

"I want two boiled eggs, one of them so undercooked it's runny, and the other so overcooked that it's tough and hard to eat. Also, I want grilled bacon that has been left on the plate to get cold, burnt toast that crumbles into nothing as soon as you touch it with a knife, butter straight from the deep freeze so that it's impossible to spread and a pot of very weak coffee, lukewarm."

"That's a complicated order, sir," says the bewildered waiter. "It might be quite difficult."

The guest replies, "Oh, but that's what you gave me yesterday!"

Careful Driver

As a trucker is sitting at a red light, a blonde driving a car stops behind him. She jumps out of her car, runs up to his truck and knocks on the window. The trucker lowers the window, and she says "Hi. My name is Heather, and you're losing some of your load."

The trucker ignores her and proceeds down the street. When the truck stops at another red light, the young woman catches up to him again. She jumps out of her car, runs up and knocks on the window. Again, the trucker lowers the window.

As if they've never spoken, the blonde says brightly, "Hello. My name is Heather, and I notice that you're losing some of your load!"

Shaking his head, the trucker ignores her again and continues down the street. At the third red light, the same thing happens again. All out of breath, the blonde gets out of her car and runs up to the truck. The trucker lowers the window. Again she says, "Hi. My name is Heather, and you are losing some of your load!"

When the light turns green, the trucker revs up and races to the next light. When he stops this time, he quickly gets out of his truck and runs back to the blonde. He knocks on her window, and as she lowers it, he says "Hi. My name is Kevin. It's winter in Edmonton, and I'm driving the sanding truck!"

Hitchhiker

Sally is driving home from one of her business trips in northern BC when she sees an elderly Native woman walking on the side of the road. As her trip has been a long and quiet one, Sally stops the car and asks the woman if she would like a ride. With a word of thanks, the old woman gets in the car.

After resuming the journey and a bit of small talk, the Native woman notices a large brown bag on the seat next to Sally.

"What's in the bag?" asks the old woman.

Sally looks down at the bag and says, "It's a two-four. Got it for my husband."

The Native woman is silent for a moment then says with the quiet wisdom of an elder, "Good trade."

Q: Why are the obese angry at the Supreme Court of Canada for giving them extra seats when they fly Air Canada or WestJet?

A: Because they really wanted extra meals!

Flight Fright!

A plane is taking off from Toronto's Pearson International Airport. After it reaches a comfortable cruising altitude, the captain makes an announcement over the intercom. "Ladies and gentlemen, this is your captain speaking. Welcome to flight number 198, non-stop from Toronto to Winnipeg. The weather ahead is good, and we should have a smooth flight. Please sit back, relax and...my goodness!"

There is silence over the intercom.

A few moments later, the captain comes back on the intercom and says, "Ladies and gentlemen, I'm so sorry if I scared you earlier, but while I was talking, the flight attendant brought me a cup of hot coffee and accidently spilled it in my lap. You should see the front of my pants!"

A passenger in coach yells, "That's nothing. He should see the back of mine!"

Riding Horseback

A woman from Toronto is driving through a remote part of western Alberta when her car breaks down. A young Native guy on horseback passes by and offers her a ride to the closest town. She accepts his offer, hops up behind him on the horse and they ride off.

The ride is uneventful except that every few minutes, the guy lets out a "Yeeeehaaaaa!" so loud that it echoes from the surrounding hills.

When they arrive in town, he drops off the woman at the local gas station. Before he leaves, he yells one final, "Yeeeeehaaaaaa!" and rides off.

"What did you do to get that Indian so excited?" asks the gas jockey.

"Nothing. I just sat behind him on the horse, put my arms around his waist and held onto his saddle horn so I wouldn't fall off."

"Lady," the attendant says, "Indians ride bare-back."

Saved

A depressed young woman is so despondent that she decides to end her life by throwing herself into the ocean. When she goes down to the docks, a handsome young sailor notices her tears, takes pity on her and says, "Look, you've got a lot to live for. I'm off to Europe in the morning, and if you like, I can stow you away on my ship. I'll take good care of you and bring you food every day." Moving closer, he slips his arm around her shoulder and says, "I'll keep you happy, and you'll keep me happy."

The girl nods yes; after all, what does she have to lose? That night, the sailor takes her aboard and hides her in a lifeboat. During the voyage, he brings her three sandwiches and a piece of fruit every night, and afterwards they make passionate love until dawn.

Three weeks later, during a routine inspection, the captain discovers the woman's hiding place. "What are you doing here?" the captain asks her.

The woman stands up and explains the situation to the captain. "I have an arrangement with one of the sailors. He's taking me to Europe, and he's screwing me."

The captain looks at her quizzically and says, "He sure is, lady. This is the Vancouver Island Ferry."

Old-timer Field Trip

A senior citizens' group charters a bus from Toronto to Québec City at night. As the bus leaves the outskirts of the city, an elderly woman walks up to the driver and says, "I've just been molested!"

The driver believes his passenger must have fallen asleep and had a bad dream. So he tells her to please return to her seat and sit down.

Five minutes later, another old woman comes forward and claims she was just molested. The driver thinks he has a busload of old wackos because who would molest those old ladies?

About 10 minutes later, a third old lady comes up and says that she's been molested too. The bus driver decides that he has had enough and pulls into the first rest area he sees.

When he turns the interior lights on and stands up, he sees an old man on his hands and knees crawling in the aisle.

"Hey, gramps, what are you doing down there?" says the bus driver.

"I lost my toupee. I thought I found it three times, but every time I go to grab it, it runs away."

Natural Obstacles

Three men are walking along a wilderness trail in northern BC and come upon a wide and raging river. They want to get to the other side of the river but have no idea of how to go about it.

The first man prays to God saying, "Please, God, give me the strength to cross this river." Poof! God gives him muscular arms and strong legs, and the man is able to swim across the river in about three hours.

Seeing this, the second man prays to God saying, "Please, God, give me the strength and ability to cross this river. Poof! A rowboat appears, and the man is able to row across the river in about two hours.

Q: What do you call a sophisticated American?

A: Canadian.

The third man has seen how this worked out for the other two men, so he also prays to God saying "Please, God, give me the strength, ability and intelligence to cross this river." Poof! God turns him into a woman. She looks at the map and walks across the bridge.

Travel Expenses

A husband and wife are travelling by car from Toronto to Calgary. After almost 24 hours on the road, they decide to stop at a nice hotel and book a room. They plan to sleep for only four hours and then get back on the road. When they check out four hours later, the desk clerk hands them a bill for $350.

The man explodes in anger and demands to know why the charge is so high. He tells the clerk although it's a nice hotel, the rooms certainly aren't worth $350. When the clerk explains that $350 is the standard rate, the man insists on speaking to the manager.

The manager appears and explains that the hotel has an Olympic-sized pool and a huge conference centre that were available for the couple to use. He also explains that they could have taken in one of the shows that the hotel is famous for. "The best entertainers from New York, Hollywood and Las Vegas perform here," says the manager.

No matter what facility the manager mentions, the man replies, "But we didn't use it!"

The manager is unmoved. Eventually, the man gives up and agrees to pay. He writes a cheque and hands it to the manager.

"But sir," says the manager, "this cheque is made out for only $100."

"That's right," replies the man. "I charged you $250 for sleeping with my wife."

"What! I didn't sleep with your wife!" exclaims the manager.

"Well," the man replies, "she was here, and you could have."

Money Talks

A subway car is packed during rush hour in Toronto, and many people are forced to stand. One particularly cramped woman turns to the man behind her and says, "Sir, if you don't stop poking me with your thing, I'm going to call the cops!"

"I don't know what you're talking about, Miss. That's just my paycheque in my pocket."

"Oh, really?" she replies. "That must be some job you have because that's the fifth raise you've had in the last 15 minutes!"

Retirement Planning

Jacob, 92, and Rebecca, 89, live in Victoria and are excited about their decision to get married. They go for a stroll to discuss the wedding, and on the way they pass a drugstore. Jacob suggests they go in.

Jacob addresses the man behind the counter.

Jacob: "Are you the owner?"

Pharmacist: "Yes."

Jacob: "We're about to get married. Do you sell heart medication?"

Pharmacist: "Yes, of course we do."

Jacob: "How about medicine for circulation?"

Pharmacist: "Yes, we provide all kinds."

Jacob: "What about medicine for rheumatism and scoliosis?"

Pharmacist: "Definitely."

Jacob: "How about Viagra?"

Pharmacist: "Of course."

Jacob: "Medicine for memory problems, arthritis and incontinence?"

Pharmacist: "Yes, we have a large variety—the works."

Jacob: "What about vitamins, sleeping pills, Geritol and drugs for Parkinson's disease?"

Pharmacist: "Absolutely."

Jacob: "You sell wheelchairs and walkers?"

Pharmacist: "Yes, all types and sizes."

Jacob: "Great! We'd like to use this store as our Bridal Registry."

Leave a Good Tip

A Montréaler stops by a local café for breakfast. After paying his tab, he checks his pockets and leaves a tip for his waitress—three pennies.

As he strides toward the door, his waitress muses, only half to herself, "You know, you can tell a lot about a man by the tip he leaves."

The man turns around, curiosity getting the better of him. "Oh, really? Tell me, what does my tip say about me?"

"Well, this penny tells me you're a thrifty man."

Barely able to conceal his pride, the man utters, "Hmm, true enough."

"And this second penny tells me you're a bachelor."

Surprised at the young woman's perception, the man says, "Well, that's true, too."

"And the third penny tells me that your father was also one."

Overheard at a Québec City Restaurant

Customer: "Waiter, waiter! There's a frog in my soup!"

Waiter: "Bon appétit!"

Canadian Fable

An old farmer, a boy and a donkey are going into town, and the old man decides that the boy should ride the donkey. As they walk along, they pass some folks who tell them it's a shame for the boy to ride and the old man to walk. The old man and boy decide that maybe the critics are right, so they change positions.

Later, they pass some more people who think that it's a real shame for the man to make such a small boy walk. The two decide that maybe they both should walk.

Soon the old man and the boy pass some other people who think it's stupid for the old man and boy to walk when they have a donkey to ride. The man and the boy decide maybe the critics are right, so they decide that they both should ride the donkey.

They soon pass other people who think it's a shame to put such a heavy load on a poor little animal. The old man and the boy decide that maybe the critics are right, so they decide to carry the donkey.

As they are crossing a bridge, the old man and the boy lose their grip on the donkey and it falls into the river and drowns.

The moral of the story: If you try to please everyone, you will eventually lose your ass.

Chapped Lips

A young cowboy rides into Calgary for the Stampede on his brand-new horse and ties it to a post. He then lifts the horse's tail and kisses its back end. An old man sees what the stranger has done and asks why he just kissed the horse's rear end.

"It helps my chapped lips," replies the cowboy.

"You mean kissing a horse's ass cures 'em?" asks the old man.

"It doesn't cure 'em," replies the cowboy. "But it stops me from licking them."

Making Friends on a Plane

A man and a woman are seated next to each other in first class on an Air Canada flight from Montréal to France. The man sneezes, pulls out his wang and wipes the tip off. The woman can't believe what she just saw and decides she must be hallucinating.

Q: Why aren't there any Mexicans in Canada?

A: They can't run that far.

A few minutes pass, and the man sneezes again. He again pulls out his wang and wipes the tip off. The woman is about to go nuts. She can't believe that such a rude person exists.

Several minutes later, the man sneezes yet again. He takes his wang out and wipes the tip off. The woman has finally had enough. She turns to the man and says, "Three times you've sneezed, and three times you've removed your penis from your pants to wipe it off! What the hell kind of degenerate are you?"

The man replies, "I am sorry to have disturbed you, ma'am. I have a very rare condition such that when I sneeze, I have an orgasm."

The woman says, "Oh, how strange. What are you taking for it?"

The man looks at her and says, "Pepper."

Native Instincts

A tour bus filled with Japanese tourists is roaming through the legendary wilderness in northern

Alberta. The tour guide tells the passengers fanciful tales of the Old West and of the famous Natives back then. One passenger wants to hear more about the Natives, and the guide explains that they were excellent trackers.

"A Native man can track a man or animal over land, through air, even under water," explains the guide to his captivated audience. One of the tourists turns to another and begins talking excitedly about the Natives and their mystical powers.

No sooner does he say this than the tour bus rounds a corner, and there in the middle of the road lies a Native guy. He has one ear pressed to the road, with his right leg held high in the air. The tour bus stops, and the passengers gather around the prostrate man, with cameras in hand, snapping pictures for friends back home.

"What are you tracking? What are you listening for?" inquires the tour guide, hoping that the Native guy will back up his story.

"Down the road, about 60 kilometres, is a red 1986 Chevy pickup," replies the Native guy. "The back tires are bald. The front end is out of whack, and the truck has dents all over it. There are a bunch of Native guys in the back and two dogs in the front seat."

The tour guide looks at his passengers, and they are all amazed.

"My God, man, how do you know all of this?" asks the guide.

The Native guy replies, "I fell out of the bloody thing about an hour ago."

On the Train

On a Calgary-bound train, three businessmen and a ravishing young woman wearing a long dress are sitting in one compartment. The four passengers engage in conversation, which very soon turns to the erotic.

The beautiful young woman makes a proposal. "If each of you guys give me one dollar, I'll show you my legs."

The men, charmed by the young woman, all give her a loonie.

The woman pulls up her dress a bit to show them the calves of her legs. Then she says, "If each of you gentlemen will give me $10, I'll show you my thighs."

The men, being what they are, each pull out a 10-dollar bill and hand it over to her.

The woman pulls up her dress all the way to reveal her legs in their full splendour.

The conversation continues, and the men, a bit excited, take off their jackets.

The young woman says, "If you all give me $100, I'll show you where I was operated on for my appendicitis."

All three men quickly fork over the money. The woman then turns to the window and points outside at a building they're passing. "See, there in the distance? That's the hospital where I had it done!"

Made in Japan

A Japanese tourist is in Toronto to do some sightseeing. On the last day of his trip, he hails a cab and tells the driver to go to the airport. During the journey, a Honda car drives past the taxi. The Japanese man rolls down his window, leans out and yells excitedly to the taxi driver, "Honda, very fast! Made in Japan!"

After a while, a Toyota speeds past the taxi. Again, the Japanese man leans out of the window and yells, "Toyota, very fast! Made in Japan!"

And then a Mitsubishi drives by the taxi. For the third time, the Japanese leans out of the window and yells, "Mitsubishi, very fast! Made in Japan!"

The taxi driver is getting a little angry, but he keeps quiet. This goes on for several more cars. Finally, the taxi arrives at the airport. The fare is $300.

The Japanese exclaims, "Wah! So expensive!"

The taxi driver turns to his passenger and yells back, "Meter, very fast! Made in Japan!"

CHAPTER TWELVE
A Canadian and Justice

Criminal Necessity

In a Montréal court room, the defendant is brought in handcuffs before a judge to answer for his crimes.

"Sir, I understand you admit to having broken into the dress shop four times," the judge says.

"Yes, Your Honour," the man replies.

"What did you steal?" the judge asks.

"I stole a dress, Your Honour," replies the man.

"One dress?" the judge bellows. "But you have admitted to breaking into the dress shop *four* times."

"Yes, that's true, Your Honour," says the suspect with a sigh, "but the first three times my wife didn't like the colour!"

The Whole Truth

A slimy Toronto lawyer defending a man accused of burglary tries this creative defence: "My client merely inserted his arm into the window and removed a few trifling articles. His arm is not himself, and I fail to see how you can punish the whole individual for an offence committed by his limb."

"Well put," the judge replies. "Using your logic, I sentence the defendant's arm to one year's imprisonment. He can accompany it or not, as he chooses."

The defendant smiles. With his lawyer's assistance, he detaches his artificial limb, lays it on the bench and walks out.

Bridge Cop

Bob, a lawyer, is driving home over Montréal's Champlain Bridge after spending a great day on the water fishing. His catch, cleaned and filleted, is wrapped in newspaper on the passenger-side floor. He is late getting home and steps on the gas. Suddenly, a cop jumps out into the road, radar gun in hand and motions him to the side of the bridge. Bob pulls over like a responsible citizen.

The cop walks up to the window and says, "You know how fast you were going, mister?"

Bob thinks for a second and says, "Uh…60?"

"Sixty-eight kilometres per hour, son, in a 55 zone!" says the cop.

"But if you already knew that, officer," replies Bob, "why did you ask me?"

Fuming over Bob's answer, the officer growls and says in a sarcastic fashion, "That's speeding, and you're getting a ticket and a fine!"

The cop takes a good close look at Bob in his stained fishing attire and says, "You don't even look like you have a job! Why, I've never seen anyone so scruffy in my entire life!"

Bob replies, "I have job! A good, well-paying job as a matter of fact!"

The cop leans in the window, smells Bob's fish and says, "Really? What kind of job would a bum like you have?"

"I'm a rectum stretcher," replies Bob.

"What did you say, boy?" says the officer.

"I'm a rectum stretcher," Bob says.

The cop, scratching his head, asks, "What does a rectum stretcher do?"

Bob replies, "People call me up and say they need to be stretched, so I go over to their house. I start with a couple of fingers, then a couple more, then one whole hand and then two. Then I slowly pull the rectum farther and farther apart until it's a full six feet across."

The cop, absorbed with this bizarre image in his mind, asks, "What the hell do you do with a six-foot asshole?"

Bob replies, "You give him a radar gun and place him by a bridge!"

Silly Question

A tourist visiting Montréal asks a man in uniform, "Are you a police officer?"

"No, I'm an undercover detective."

"So why are you in uniform?"

"Today is my day off."

City Lawyer vs. Farmer

A big city Toronto lawyer goes duck hunting in rural Alberta. He shoots and kills a bird, but it lands in a farmer's field on the other side of a fence. As the lawyer is climbing over the fence, an elderly farmer drives up on his tractor and asks the guy what he is doing.

The lawyer replies, "I shot a duck, and it fell in this field, and now I'm going to retrieve it."

The old farmer says, "This is my property, and you are not coming over here."

"I'm one of the best trial attorneys in Canada," the lawyer says. "And if you don't let me get that duck, I'll sue you and take everything you own."

The old farmer smiles and says, "Apparently you don't know how we settle disputes in Alberta. We settle small disagreements like this with the 'Three Kick Rule.'"

The lawyer asks, "What is the Three Kick Rule?"

"Well, because the dispute occurs on my land," replies the farmer, "first, I kick you three times and then you kick me three times and so on, back and forth until someone gives up."

The lawyer quickly thinks about the proposed contest and decides that he could easily take the old codger. He agrees to abide by the local custom.

The old farmer slowly climbs down from the tractor and walks up to the lawyer. With his first kick, the farmer plants the toe of his heavy steel-toed work boot into the lawyer's groin.

The lawyer drops to the ground, writhing in pain. The second kick to the midriff sends the lawyer's last meal gushing from his mouth. The lawyer is on all fours when the farmer's third kick to his rear end sends him face-first into a fresh cow pie.

The lawyer summons every last bit of his strength and manages to get to his feet. Wiping his face with the arm of his jacket, he says, "Okay. Now it's my turn."

The old farmer smiles and says, "Naw, I give up. You can have the duck."

Border Smarts

Five Americans in an Audi Quattro arrive at a Québec–Canadian border checkpoint.

Pierre, the customs officer, stops them and says, "It's illegal to put five people in a Quattro."

"What do you mean it's *illegal*?" asks the American.

"*Quattro* means four," replies Pierre.

"Quattro is just the name of the car," the American retorts disbelievingly. "Look at the papers! It says, 'This car is designed to carry five persons.'"

"You can't pull that one on me," replies Pierre. "*Quattro* means four. You have five people in your vehicle, and you are therefore breaking the law."

The American replies angrily, "You idiot! Call your supervisor over. I want to speak to someone with more intelligence!"

"Sorry," responds Pierre, "Jean-Luc is busy with two guys in a Fiat Uno."

Supreme Lawyer

Walking past the Supreme Court of Canada one day, a man spots a friend of his sitting on the steps outside, sobbing loudly with his head buried in his hands.

"What's the matter?" he asks his friend. "Did your lawyer give you bad advice?"

"No, it's worse than that," replies the friend between sobs. "He sold it to me."

Choose Carefully

An Albertan, a Quebecker and a Newfie are arrested and convicted of murder.

At their sentencing hearing, the judge tells them they will be locked up in solitary for 50 years, but that he'll allow each of them one item.

The Albertan says he wants beer, so he goes into his cell with all the booze he wants.

The Quebecker says he wants some women, so he goes in with his women.

The Newfie wants cigarettes, so he goes in with his cigarettes.

Fifty years later, the three men are freed. The Albertan comes out of jail piss drunk, the Quebecker comes out with his women and several kids, and the Newfie comes out and says, "Anybody got a light?"

Clean Record

A Calgary police officer stops a car that is swerving all over the road. The driver is obviously intoxicated, but since the guy has a clean record, the officer makes him park the car and takes the man home in his police car.

"Are you sure this is your house?" the cop asks as they drive into a rather upscale neighbourhood.

"Shertainly!" says the drunk, "and if you'll just open the door f'me, I can prove it to ya." Entering the living room, the man says, "You shee that piano? Thash mine. You shee that giant television shet? Thast mine too. Now follow me."

The police officer follows the man as he shakily negotiates the stairs to the second floor. The drunk opens the first door they come to. "Thish ish my bedroom," he announces. "Shee the bed there? Thast mine! Shee that woman lying in the bed? Thash my wife. An' see that guy lying next to her?"

"Yeah…" the cop replies suspiciously as he is beginning at this point to seriously doubt the man's story.

"Well, thash me!"

Air Justice

A man is just settling into his window seat on a plane when another man sits down in the aisle seat and puts his black Labrador retriever on the middle seat between them.

The first man asks why the dog is allowed in the passenger area.

The second man explains that he is an RCMP officer and that the dog is a sniffing dog. "His name is Sniffer, and he's the best there is," he says. "I'll show you once we get airborne how I put him to work."

The plane takes off, and once it has levelled out, the agent says, "Watch this." He tells Sniffer to "search."

Sniffer jumps down from his seat, walks along the aisle and purposely sits next to a woman for several seconds. Sniffer then returns to his seat and puts one paw on the officer's arm.

The officer says, "Good boy." He turns to the other man and says, "That woman is in possession of marijuana, so I'm making a note of her seat number. The authorities will apprehend her when we land."

"Say, that's pretty neat," replies the first man.

Once again, the officer sends Sniffer to search the aisle. The dog sniffs around, sits down beside a man for a few seconds, returns to his seat and places two paws on the officer's arm. The officer says, "That man is carrying cocaine, so again, I'm making a note of his seat number for the police."

The agent then tells Sniffer to search again. The obedient dog walks up and down the aisle for a little while, sits down for a moment and then comes racing back to the officer. Sniffer jumps into the middle seat and proceeds to poop all over the place.

The first man is really disgusted by this behaviour and can't figure out why a well-trained RCMP dog would act like that, so he asks the officer, "What's going on?"

The officer nervously replies, "He just found a bomb!"

CHAPTER THIRTEEN

A Strange Canadian

Odd Encounter

A beaver is approached by a prostitute. Since he has never been with one before, he is curious and excited. They spend the night together in a hotel having sex, and he goes down on her the next morning one last time before he leaves.

As he is heading for the door, the prostitute yells, "Hey, what about my money?"

The beaver turns, gives her a puzzled look and shrugs his shoulders.

She says, "Come here," and pulls out a small dictionary from her purse. She points to the word "prostitute" and its definition: "Has sex and gets paid."

Finally understanding, the beaver grabs the dictionary, finds the word "beaver" and shows her the definition: "Eats bush and leaves."

Bad News?

An old guy from Labrador goes to the doctor for his annual check-up.

The doctor says, "Well, Mr. Jones, I have bad news, and I have worse news."

The guy thinks for a few seconds then says, "Gimme the worst news first."

"Well, Mr. Jones," the doctor says, "I'm sorry to have to tell you this, but you have cancer."

The man says, "That's terrible news! And what's the bad news?"

The doc says, "Well, Mr. Jones, you also have Alzheimer's disease."

"Well," replies Mr. Jones, "at least I don't have cancer!"

Out Shopping

A Newfie blind man walks into a department store with his seeing-eye dog. All of a sudden, he picks up the dog's leash and starts to swing the dog over his head.

The store security guard runs up to the man and asks, "What the hell are you doing?"

The blind man replies, "Just looking around."

Q: How was copper wire invented?

A: Two Canadians were fighting over a penny.

Out of Sorts

A businessman from Calgary has had a headache for 20 years and is at the point where he wants to end his own life, but he decides to see some specialists first.

No doctor can solve his problem, until finally one of them says, "You have a very rare condition. Your testicles are pressed up against your spine, causing your headaches. The only way to remedy it is to remove your testicles."

The man hesitantly agrees and gets them removed right then and there.

On his way home, he walks past a tailor shop that is displaying a sign saying, "All Suits Half Price."

Being in need of a new suit, he walks in and is greeted by a man who says, "Hello, sir, I see you want a suit. I would say that you are a 34 sleeve and a 24 pant."

"Wow! How did you know that?" says the man.

"Why, sir, I've been in this business for 40 years. Would you like shoes to go with your suit?"

"Sure," replies the man.

"Okay, I'd say that you're a size 10 wide."

"Wow, now you're freaking me out! That's a great talent," says the man.

"Thanks," the shopkeeper replies. "Now, how about some undergarments?"

"Okay, see if you can guess my size," says the man.

"Easy. It's 36," says the shopkeeper.

"Nope. It's 34," replies the man.

The shopkeeper exclaims, "Impossible! A size 34 would squish your testicles against your spine, giving you a terrible headache."

Mail Box

In a quiet suburban Ottawa neighbourhood, George is mowing the grass in his front yard when his blonde female neighbour, Bonnie, comes out of her house and heads straight to her mailbox. She opens it, then slams it shut and storms back into the house.

A little later she comes out of her house again, gets to the mailbox, and again opens it and slams it shut again. Angrily, Bonnie goes back into her house.

As George is getting ready to edge his lawn, Bonnie comes out again, marches to the mailbox opens it and then slams it close harder than ever.

Puzzled by her actions George asks her, "Is something wrong?"

To which Bonnie replies, "There certainly is! My stupid computer keeps saying, 'You've got mail.'"

Getting Even

For decades, two heroic statues in Ottawa, one male and one female, faced each other in a park. One day an angel comes down from heaven and approaches the statues.

"You've been such great statues," the angel says, "so I am going to give you the gift of life for 30 minutes. In that time, you may do anything you want." And with a clap of his hands, the two statues come to life.

The two statues walk slowly toward each other, stare deep into each other's eyes and immediately run into the bushes, where a great deal of giggling can be heard through the shaking branches.

Fifteen minutes later, the two statues emerge from the bushes with huge grins on their faces.

"You still have 15 more minutes," says the angel with a wink.

Grinning, the male statue says to the female, "Great! Okay, this time you hold down the pigeon, and I'll shit on his head."

Shortest Canadian Book:
Québec Hospitality

Doctor in the House

Two Newfies are sitting in a restaurant. While having a bite to eat, they talk about their upcoming fishing trip.

Suddenly, a woman at a nearby table, who is eating a sandwich, begins to cough. After a few seconds, it becomes apparent that she is in real distress. One of the Newfies walks up to her and says, "Can ya swalluh?"

The woman shakes her head no.

Then he asks, "Can ya breathe?"

The woman begins to turn blue and shakes her head no.

The Newfie lifts up her dress, yanks down her drawers and quickly gives her right butt cheek a lick with his tongue. The woman is so shocked that she has a violent spasm, and the obstruction flies out of her mouth.

As she begins to breathe again, the Newfie slowly walks back to his table.

His partner says, "Ya know, I heard of dat 'Hind Lick Manoeuvre,' but I never see'd nobody do it, b'y!"

Construction Workers

An Italian, an Irishman and a Chinese fellow start their new jobs at a Montréal construction site.

The foreman points to a huge pile of sand and says to the Italian guy, "You're in charge of sweeping."

To the Irishman he says, "You're in charge of shovelling."

To the Chinese guy, "You're in charge of supplies."

The foreman then says, "Now, I have to leave for a little while. I expect you guys to make a dent in that pile of sand."

When the foreman returns to the site a few hours later, the pile of sand is untouched.

He says to the Italian, "Why didn't you sweep any of it?"

The Italian replies in a heavy accent, "I no gotta broom, an' you tella me dat de Chinese'a guy supposa bringa da supplies, but he disappear and I no finda him."

Then the foreman turns to the Irishman and asks why he didn't shovel.

The Irishman replies in his heavy brogue, "Aye, that ye did, but I couldna get meself a shovel. Ye left the Chinese fella in charge of supplies, but I couldna fin' him."

The foreman is really angry now and storms off searching for the Chinese guy.

He can't find him anywhere and is getting angrier by the minute. Just then, the Chinese guy springs out from behind the pile of sand and yells, "Supplies!"

A Dog Named "Sex"

"Why exactly are you here in court, sir?" a judge asks the defendant.

"Well, a lot of dog owners in Vancouver name their dogs 'Rover' or 'Boy,'" replies the man. "I call mine 'Sex.' Now, Sex has been very embarrassing to me. When I went to renew his dog licence, I told the clerk I would like to have a licence for Sex.

"He said, 'I'd like to have one too.' Then I said, 'But this is a dog.'

"He said he didn't care what she looked like.

"Then I said, 'You don't understand. I've had Sex since I was nine years old.'

"He said I must have been quite a kid!

"When I got married and went on my honeymoon, I took the dog with me. I told the motel clerk that I wanted a room for my wife and me, and a special room for Sex. He said that every room in the place was for sex. I said, 'You don't understand. Sex keeps me awake at night.'

"The clerk said, 'Me too.'

"One day, I entered Sex in a contest, but before the competition began, the dog ran away. Another contestant asked me why I was just standing there, looking around. I told him I had planned to have Sex in the contest. He told me that I should have sold my own tickets.

"'But you don't understand,' I said, 'I had hoped to have Sex on TV.'

"He called me a show-off.

"When my wife and I separated, we went to court to fight for custody of the dog. I said, 'Your Honour, I had Sex before I was married.'

"The judge said, 'Me too.'

"Then I told him that after I was married, Sex left me.

"He said, 'Me too.' I got custody of Sex.

"Last night, Sex ran off again. I spent hours looking around town for him. A cop came over to me and asked, 'What are you doing in this alley at four o'clock in the morning?'

I said, 'I'm looking for Sex.' And that's why I'm in court today."

Blonde in a Bank

A blonde walks into a bank in Toronto and asks for the loan officer. She says she's going to Europe on business for two weeks and needs to borrow $5000. The bank officer says the bank will need some kind of security for the loan, so the blonde hands over the keys to a new Rolls Royce. The car is parked on the street in front of the bank, she has the title and everything checks out. The bank agrees to accept the car as collateral for the loan.

The bank's president and its officers all enjoy a good laugh at the blonde for using a $250,000 Rolls Royce as collateral against a $5000 loan. An employee of the bank then proceeds to drive the Rolls into the bank's underground garage and parks it there.

Two weeks later, the blonde returns, repays the $5000 and the interest, which comes to $15.41. The loan officer says, "Miss, we are very happy to have had your business, and this transaction has worked out very nicely, but we are a little puzzled. While you were away, we checked you out and found that you are a multimillionaire. What puzzles us is, why would you bother to borrow $5000?"

The blonde replies, "Where else in Toronto can I park my car for two weeks for only $15.41 and expect it to be there when I return?"

Canadian Blonde on a Plane

On a plane bound for Fredericton, the flight attendant approaches a blonde sitting in the first-class section and requests that she moves to coach since she does not have a first-class ticket.

The blonde replies, "I'm blonde, I'm beautiful, I'm going to Fredericton and I'm not moving."

Not wanting to argue with a customer, the flight attendant asks the co-pilot to speak with the unco-operative passenger.

He goes to talk with the woman asking her to please move out of the first-class section.

Again, the blonde replies, "I'm blonde, I'm beautiful, I'm going to Fredericton and I'm not moving."

The co-pilot returns to the cockpit and asks the captain what he should do.

The captain says, "I'm married to a blonde, and I know how to handle this." He goes to the first-class section and whispers in the blonde's ear. She immediately jumps up and runs to the coach section mumbling to herself, "Why didn't anyone just say so?"

Surprised, the flight attendant and the co-pilot ask what he said to her that finally convinced her to move from her seat.

He says, "I told her the first-class section wasn't going to Fredericton."

Special Elevator

A Newfie family are visiting a big city for the first time. The father and son are in the hotel lobby when they spot an elevator.

"What's dat, Dad?" the boy asks, pointing to the elevator.

"I did never did see nothin' like dat in my life," replies the father.

Seconds later an old frail woman walks into the hotel and hobbles to the elevator. She presses the button with her cane, waits for the doors to open and gets in.

The father and son, still amazed by this contraption, continue to watch.

They hear a ping noise, and the elevator doors open again. Out steps a beautiful 20-year-old blonde.

The Newfie father looks at his son and says, "Quick! Go git yer mother!"

At the Vet

Dr. Adams is the local veterinarian in Victoria, and he is known for his wry humour. He surpasses himself one summer day when a dog is brought to him after an encounter with a porcupine.

After almost an hour of prying, pulling, cutting and stitching, he returns the dog to its owner, a tourist, who asks what she owes him.

"Fifty dollars, Ma'am," he answers.

"Why, that's simply outrageous!" she yells. "That's what's wrong with you Victoria people; you're always trying to overcharge summer visitors. What do you do in the winter, when you're not overcharging your clients?"

"Raise porcupines, Ma'am."

Sound Advice

An insurance salesman from Toronto makes a trip out to a rural community to sell insurance to the farmers. He is way out in the country when he has engine trouble. Not knowing anything about cars, he gets out and looks under the hood anyway.

All of a sudden he hears a voice that says, "It's the carburettor."

The insurance man jumps and looks around, seeing no one. He then looks under the hood again, hoping it is something visible he can fix himself, when he hears the voice again, "It's the carbonator."

The man jumps again and turns around only seeing a large bull behind him. Scared out of his wits, he takes off running to the nearest farmhouse he can find.

He knocks on the door, the farmer answers, and the man immediately goes into his story about the bull.

The farmer scratches his head and says, "Did the bull have one straight ear and one floppy ear?"

The man nods and says, "Yes, Yes. That's it."

The farmer laughs and says, "Oh, don't worry about him. He doesn't know as much about cars as he thinks he does."

Cough Remedy

The owner of a drugstore in Kelowna walks in to find a customer leaning heavily against the back wall. The owner asks the new clerk, "What's with that guy over there by the wall?"

The clerk says, "Well, he came in here this morning to get something for his cough. I couldn't find the cough syrup, so I gave him a bottle of laxative."

The store owner says, "You idiot! You can't treat a cough with a laxative!"

"Oh yeah?" replies the clerk. "Look at him—he's afraid to cough!"

Thankful Billionaire

An Albertan billionaire falls ill. The doctors he consults don't know what's wrong with him. The billionaire lets it be known that if any doctor can heal him, he'll give that doctor whatever he desires.

A rural doctor is finally able to cure the rich man, and as the doctor is leaving, the Albertan says, "Doc! I'm a man of my word. You name it, and if it is humanly possible, I'll get it for you."

"Well," says the doctor, "I love to play golf, so if I could have a matching set of golf clubs, that would be fine." With that, the physician leaves.

The doctor doesn't hear from the billionaire for some months. Then, one day, he gets a phone call from the rich Albertan.

"Doc, I bet you thought that I had gone back on my word. I have your matching set of golf clubs. The reason it took so long is that two of them didn't have swimming pools, and I didn't think they were good enough for you, after all you've done for me. So I had the pools installed, and your clubs are all ready for you now!"

The Queen Visits a Hospital

Queen Elizabeth II is visiting one of Halifax's finest hospitals, and during her tour of the wards, she passes a room where one of the male patients is masturbating.

"Oh God!" exclaims the Queen, "that's disgraceful! What is the meaning of this?"

The doctor leading the tour explains, "I'm sorry, your Royal Highness, but this man has a serious medical condition that causes his testicles to fill up rapidly with semen. If he doesn't do what he is doing at least five times per day, he could swell up and die."

"Oh, I'm sorry," replies the Queen. "I was unaware that such a medical condition existed."

On the same floor, they soon pass another room where a young blonde nurse is performing oral sex on another patient.

"Oh, my God!" exclaims the Queen. "What's happening here?"

The doctor replies, "Same problem, better health plan."

Probably a True Story

Once upon a time there lived a woman in rural Alberta who had a maddening passion for baked beans. She loved them, but unfortunately they had an embarrassing and somewhat lively reaction for her.

One day she meets a guy at a party and falls in love. When they decide to marry, she thinks to herself, "He is such a sweet and gentle man; he would never go for this carrying on." So she makes the supreme sacrifice and gives up eating beans after they get married.

Q: Why did the Newfie cross the road?

A: I don't know. Neither did he.

Some months later, her car breaks down on the way home from work. She calls her husband and tells him that she will be late because she has to walk home. On her walk home, she passes a small diner, and the smell of the baked beans is more than she can stand. Since she still has a few miles to walk, she figures that she could walk off any ill effects of the beans by the time she gets home. So she stops at the diner and before she knows it, she has consumed three large orders of baked beans. All the way home she putt-putts. And upon arriving home, she feels reasonably sure she can control herself.

Her husband seems excited to see her and exclaims delightedly, "Darling, I have a surprise for dinner tonight." He then blindfolds her and leads her to a chair at the dinner table. She sits down, and just as her husband is about to remove the blindfold, the telephone rings. He makes her promise not to touch the blindfold until he returns.

The baked beans she has consumed are still affecting her, and the pressure is becoming almost unbearable, so while her husband is out of the room, she seizes the opportunity, shifts her weight to one leg and lets one go. It is not only loud but the odour is like a fertilizer truck running over a skunk in front of a pulpwood mill. Still wearing the blindfold, she vigorously fans the air around her with her hand.

Keeping her ears tuned to the conversation that her husband is having in the other room, she goes on like this for another five minutes. When the farewells from the phone signal the end of her freedom, she fans the air a few more times.

She is the picture of innocence when her husband returns. He apologizes for taking so long and asks his wife if she peeked. She assures him that she has not. He removes the blindfold, and she is surprised! There are 12 dinner guests seated around the table to wish her a Happy Birthday!

A Real Newfie...

- calls you to get your phone number
- spends 20 minutes looking at the orange juice box because it says, "Concentrate"
- puts lipstick on her forehead because she wants to make up her mind
- tries to put M&Ms in alphabetical order
- sends a fax with a stamp on it
- tries to drown a fish
- thinks a quarterback is a refund
- gets locked in a grocery store and starves to death
- trips over a cordless phone
- takes a ruler to bed to see how long he sleeps
- asks for a price check at the Dollar Store
- studies for a blood test
- thinks Meow Mix is a CD for cats
- takes the number 22 bus twice when he misses the 44 bus
- moves when she hears that 90 percent of all crimes occur around the home

Secluded Life

In a tiny village on the Newfoundland coast lives an old lady who is a virgin and very proud of it. Sensing that her final days are rapidly approaching, and desiring to make sure everything is in proper order when she dies, she goes to the town's undertaker (who also happens to be the local postal clerk) to make the proper "final" arrangements.

As a last wish, she informs the undertaker that she wants the following inscription engraved on her tombstone: "Born a Virgin, Lived as a Virgin, Died a Virgin."

Not long after, the old maid dies peacefully. A few days after her funeral, while the undertaker/postal clerk is preparing the tombstone that the woman had requested, it becomes quite apparent that the tombstone she selected is much too small for the wording that she had chosen. He thinks long and hard about how he will fulfil the old maid's final request, considering the limited space available on the small piece of stone.

> **Q:** Why did the chicken cross the road?
>
> ***Captain Kirk:*** To boldly go where no chicken has gone before.

For days, he agonizes over the dilemma. But finally his experience as a postal worker allows him to come up with what he thinks is the appropriate solution to the problem. The virgin's tombstone is finally completed and duly engraved, and it reads: "Returned Unopened."

Bad Advice

Andre approaches his co-worker Carl at lunch and invites him out for a few beers after work on St. Laurent in Montréal. Carl says that his wife would never go for it because she does not allow him to go drinking with the guys after work.

Andre suggests a solution to the problem: "When you get home tonight, sneak into the house, slide down under the sheets in your bedroom, gently pull down your wife's panties and give her oral sex. Women love it, and believe me, she'll never mention that you were out late with the boys."

Carl agrees to try it, and the two men go out for a few beers after work.

Later that night, Carl sneaks into his house, slides into bed, gently removes his wife's panties and gives her oral sex. She moans and groans with pleasure, but after a while, Carl realizes he has to take a leak, so he whispers to her that he'll be right back. He gets out of bed and walks down the hall to the bathroom.

When he opens the bathroom door, he is shocked to see his wife sitting on the john.

"How did you get in here?" Carl asks in a loud voice.

"Shhh!" she replies, "you'll wake up my mother!"

CHAPTER FOURTEEN
A Canadian Goes to Ottawa

Robbery

Late one night in Ottawa, a mugger jumps a well-dressed man and holds a gun to his ribs.

"Give me your money!" the mugger demands.

The man stiffens but says indignantly, "You can't do this to me—I'm a Member of Parliament!"

"In that case," replies the robber, "give me my money!"

Politics

Shortest Canadian Book:
Stephen Harper's Guide to Working Together

A Member of Parliament spends the night with a high-class Ottawa hooker. In the morning, he leaves $1000 on the dresser.

"That's very generous, sir," says the hooker. "I usually only charge $300."

"But I spent the whole night with you," says the politician. "How do you make a living on only $300 a night?"

"It's easy," replies the hooker. "I do a lot of blackmail on the side."

Tax Man

A nervous taxpayer is unhappily conversing with a Canada Revenue tax auditor who is reviewing the man's records.

At one point, the auditor exclaims, "Mr. Fleury, we feel it is a great privilege to be allowed to live and work in Canada. As a citizen, you have an obligation to pay taxes, and we expect you to eagerly pay them with a smile."

"Thank goodness!" says Mr. Fleury, smiling from ear to ear. "I thought you were going to want me to pay with cash."

Government Science

Recent Canadian government research has shown that cigarette smoking not only impairs sexual ability, but it actually causes shrinkage of the male sex organ.

Wow! If that is true, we need to get the word out ASAP! Maybe the warning on cigarette packs should be updated to reflect this new information:

- Warning: These cigarettes are king size—how about you?
- Warning: If you don't reduce your smoking, your smoking will reduce you.
- Warning: Smoking may lead to ridicule on your honeymoon.
- Warning: Smoke rises, but you may not.

- Warning: Second-hand smoke can be harmful to children; that is, if you're capable of conceiving any.

- Warning: Cigarettes get shorter the more you puff—so do you.

- Warning: How can you enjoy a smoke afterwards if there's no before?

- Warning: The only thing left after a smoke is a dead stub.

- Warning: Don't throw lit cigarettes in the urinal—you might not have the range to put them out.

Titanic

Pierre Trudeau, Stephen Harper and Jack Layton are on the *Titanic*. As the ship starts to sink, Jack Layton heroically shouts, "Save the women!"

Stephen Harper hysterically screeches, "Screw the women!"

And Pierre Trudeau smirks and purrs, "Do we have time?"

Papal Visit

The Pope is visiting Ottawa, and Prime Minister Stephen Harper takes him out sailing on a yacht on the Ottawa River. They're admiring the sights when, all of a sudden, the Pope's hat (zucchetto) blows off his head and out into the water.

Secret service guys prepare to launch a boat to retrieve the hat, but Harper waves them off, saying, "Wait, wait. I'll take care of this. Don't worry."

Harper then steps off the yacht onto the surface of the water and walks out to the Holy Father's little hat, bends over and picks it up, then walks back to the boat and climbs aboard. He hands the hat to the Pope amid stunned silence.

The next morning, the *Ottawa Citizen* carries a story with front-page photos of the event. The banner headline reads "Harper Can't Swim."

Hot Air

A woman in a hot air balloon floating over a large lake realizes she is lost.

She lowers her altitude and spots a man in a boat below. She shouts to him, "Excuse me, can you help me? I promised a friend I would meet him an hour ago, but I don't know where I am."

The man consults his portable GPS and replies, "You're in a hot air balloon approximately 30 metres above a ground elevation of 2346 metres above sea level. You are 31 degrees, 14.97 minutes north latitude and 100 degrees, 49.09 minutes west longitude."

Shortest Canadian Book: *The Québec Guide to Honest Politicians*

She rolls her eyes and says, "You must be a Conservative."

"I am," replies the man. "How did you know?"

"Well," answers the balloonist, "everything you told me is technically correct, but I have no idea what to make of your information, and I'm still lost. Frankly, you haven't been much help to me."

The man smiles and responds, "You must be a New Democrat."

"I am," replies the balloonist. "How did you know?"

"Well," says the man, "you don't know where you are or where you're going. You've risen to where you are because of a large quantity of hot air. You made a promise that you have no idea how to keep, and you expect *me* to solve your problem. You're in *exactly* the same position you were in before we met, but somehow, now it's *my* fault."

Royal Visit

At Heathrow Airport in London, a 100-metre red carpet is stretched out to an airplane, and Prime Minister Stephen Harper walks the carpet to greet Queen Elizabeth II with a warm but dignified handshake. They ride in a 1937 silver Bentley to the edge of London where they board an open 17th-century coach that is hitched to six magnificent white horses. As they ride toward Buckingham Palace, each looking to their sides and waving to the thousands of people lining the streets, all is going well. What a glorious display of pageantry and dignity!

Shortest Canadian Book:
The Québec Guide to Federalism

Suddenly, the scene is shattered when the right rear horse lets rip one of the most horrific, earth-shattering, eye-tearing blasts of flatulence, and the coach is filled with noxious fumes.

Uncomfortable, but maintaining control, the two dignitaries do their best to ignore the whole incident, but the Queen decides that is a ridiculous manner in which to handle this embarrassing situation. She turns to Prime Minister Harper and says, "Mr. Harper, please accept my regrets. I'm sure you understand that there are some things even a Queen can't control."

Harper replies, "Your majesty, please don't give the matter another thought. You know, if you hadn't said something, I would have assumed it was one of the horses!"

Bar Politics

A man walks into a cowboy bar and orders a beer just as Stephen Harper appears on the television screen. After taking a few sips, the man looks up at the television above the bar and mumbles, "Now, there's the biggest horse's ass I've ever seen." A customer at the end of the bar quickly stands up, walks over to the man and decks him.

A few minutes later, as the man is finishing his beer, Rona Ambrose appears on the television. "She's a horse's ass too," says the man.

This time, a customer at the other end of the bar quickly stands up, walks over to him and knocks him off his stool.

"Damn it!" the man says, climbing back up to his bar stool. "This must be Conservative country!"

"Nope," the bartender replies. "Horse country!"

Harper's Doctor

Stephen Harper goes to see the doctor to get the results of his brain scan. The doctor says, "Mr. Prime Minister, I have some bad news for you. First, we have discovered that your brain has two sides: the left side and the right side..."

Q: Why did the chicken cross the road?
Stephen Harper: No comment.

Harper interrupts the doctor and says, "Well, that's normal, isn't it? I thought everybody had two sides to their brain?"

The doctor replies, "That's true, Mr. Prime Minister. But your brain is very unusual because on the left side there isn't anything right, while on the right side there isn't anything left."

A Political Lesson

Little Johnny goes to his dad and asks, "What is politics?"

The dad says, "Well, son, let me try to explain it this way: I'm the breadwinner of the family, so let's call me Capitalism. Your mom, she's the administrator of the money, so we'll call her the Government. We're here to take care of your needs, so we'll call you the People. The nanny, well, we'll consider her the Working Class. And your baby brother, we'll call him the Future. Now, think about that and see if that makes sense." The little boy goes off to bed thinking about what his dad has told him.

Later that night, Johnny hears his baby brother crying, so he gets up to check on him. He finds that the baby has severely soiled his diaper. Johnny goes to his parents' bedroom and finds his mother sound asleep. Not wanting to wake her, he goes to the nanny's room. Finding the door locked, he peeks in the keyhole and sees his father in bed with the nanny. Johnny decides to go back to bed.

The next morning, Johnny says to his father, "Dad, I think I understand the concept of politics now."

The father says, "Good, son. So tell me in your own words what you think politics is all about."

Johnny replies, "Well, while Capitalism is screwing the Working Class, the Government is sound asleep, the People are being ignored and the Future is in deep shit."

Old Age

A retired gentleman goes to the government pension office to apply for his much-needed pension money. After waiting in line for a long time, he finally reaches the counter. The woman behind the counter asks him for his driver's licence to verify his age. The man reaches into in his pocket and realizes he has left his wallet at home.

He tells the woman that he is very sorry, but he seems to have left his wallet at home. "Will I have to go home and come back now?" he asks.

The woman says, "Unbutton your shirt."

He opens his shirt, revealing a lot of curly silver hair.

She says, "That silver hair on your chest is proof enough for me," and she processes his pension application.

When he gets home, the man tells his wife about his experience at the Government of Canada office.

"You should have dropped your pants," she replies, "and you might have qualified for disability, too."

Voice of Dissension

An old man sitting in the front row at a Winnipeg town hall meeting is heckling the mayor as he delivers a long speech. Finally, the mayor can stand it no longer, so he points to the heckler and says, "Sir, will you please stand up and tell the audience what you have ever done for the good of the city?"

"Well, Mr. Mayor," the man says in a firm voice, "I voted against you in the last election."

Q: What do politicians and diapers have in common?

A: They both should be changed regularly. And for the same reason.

Guessing Game

Stephen Harper is having tea with the Queen of England at Buckingham Palace. He asks her, "Your Majesty, I admire how you run such an efficient government. Are there any tips you can give me?"

"Well," says the Queen, "the most important thing is to surround yourself with intelligent people."

Harper frowns. "But how do I know the people around me are really intelligent?"

After the Queen takes a sip of tea, she says, "Oh, that's easy. You just ask them to answer an intelligent riddle." She pushes a button on her intercom. "Please send David Cameron in here, would you?"

David Cameron walks into the room. "Yes, my Queen?"

The Queen smiles. "Answer me this, please, David. Your mother and father have a child. The child is not your brother and it is not your sister. Who is it?"

Without pausing for a moment, David Cameron replies, "Well, your Majesty, that would be me."

"Yes. Very good," says the Queen.

Harper goes back home to ask Vic Toews, his Minister of Public Safety, the same question. "Vic, answer this for me. Your mother and your father have a child. The child is not your brother and it's not your sister. Who is it?"

"I'm not sure," says Vic. "Let me get back to you on that one." He goes to his advisors and asks them the question, but none can give him an answer. Later, Vic ends up in the men's restroom and recognizes Peter MacKay's shoes in the next stall. Vic shouts, "Peter! Can you answer this for me? Your mother and father have a child, and it's not your brother or your sister. Who is it?"

Peter MacKay yells back, "That's easy. It's me!"

Vic smiles and says, "Thanks!"

Then Vic goes back to speak with Harper. "I did some research," says Vic, "and I have the answer to that riddle. It's Peter MacKay."

Harper gets up from behind his desk, stomps over to Vic and angrily yells into his face, "No, you idiot! It's David Cameron!"

At the Diner

One day Stephen Harper and Peter MacKay walk into a diner and sit down at a table. A waitress approaches them and asks if she can take their order. MacKay leans close to her and says, "Honey, can I have a quickie?"

The waitress is appalled and yells at MacKay about women's rights and storms away.

Stephen Harper then says to MacKay, "Peter, it's pronounced 'quiche.'"

Damn Taxman

At the end of the tax year, the Canada Revenue Agency sends an inspector to audit the books of a synagogue in Montréal. While the inspector is checking the books, he turns to the rabbi and says, "I notice you buy a lot of candles. What do you do with the candle drippings?"

"Good question," says the rabbi. "We save them up and send them back to the candle makers, and every now and then they send us a free box of candles."

"Oh," replies the auditor, somewhat disappointed that his unusual question has a practical answer. But he continues on, in his obnoxious way, and says, "What about all these biscuit purchases? What do you do with the crumbs?"

"Ah, yes," replies the rabbi, realizing that the inspector is trying to trap him with an unanswerable question. "We collect them and send them back to the manufacturers, and every now and then they send us a free box of holy biscuits."

"I see!" replies the auditor, thinking hard about how he can fluster the know-it-all rabbi. "Well, Rabbi," he says, "what do you do with all the leftover foreskins from the circumcisions you perform?"

"Here, too, we do not waste," replies the rabbi. "We save up all the foreskins and send them to your office, and about once a year they send us a complete prick."

Letter to the Government

Dear Canada Revenue Agency:

Enclosed you will find my 2012 tax return showing that I owe $3407 in taxes.

Please note the attached article from the *Globe and Mail* newspaper dated 12 November, wherein you will see the Department of Defence is paying $171.50 per hammer and the Navy pays $600 per toilet seat.

I am enclosing for four (4) toilet seats (valued at $2400) and six (6) hammers (valued at $1029) that I bought at Home Depot, bringing my total remittance to $3429. Please apply the overpayment of $22 to the "Prime Minister Election Fund," as noted on my return. You can do this inexpensively by sending them one (1) 1.5-inch Phillips head screwdriver (see aforementioned article from *Globe and Mail* detailing how the Department of Defence pays $22 each for 1.5-inch Phillips head screwdrivers). One screw is enclosed for your convenience.

> Shortest Canadian Book:
> *Stephen Harper Goes Wild*

It has been a pleasure to pay my tax bill this year, and I look forward to paying it again next year.

Sincerely,

A Satisfied Taxpayer

How Much?

Peter MacKay, Canadian Minister of Defence, is giving the prime minister his daily briefing during a staff meeting and concludes by saying, "Yesterday, three Brazilian soldiers were killed."

"Oh no!" Stephen Harper exclaims. "That's terrible!"

Harper's staff sits there stunned at the prime minister's display of emotion, nervously watching as Harper sits at the table with his head in his hands.

Finally, Harper looks up and says, "How many is a brazillion?"

New Drug Regulations

In pharmacology, all drugs have two names—a trade name and a generic name. For example, the trade name of Tylenol has a generic name of acetaminophen. Aleve is also called naproxen. Amoxil is called amoxicillin, and Advil is also called ibuprofen.

The Government of Canada has been looking for a more colloquial name for Viagra. After careful consideration by a team of federal government experts, it has been recently announced that all drugs should be named after what they do or are prescribed for. For example, Viagra, Cialis and their generic brands will be so named

Longest Canadian Book: *Stephen Harper's Quilt Patterns*

mycoxafloppin. Also considered were mycoxa-failin, mydixadrupin, mydixarizin, mydixadud, dixafix and, of course, ibepokin.

Harper's Ladies

In Ottawa, Stephen Harper is walking along looking for a call girl. Along Bank Street, he finds three such women in a local pub: a blonde, a brunette and a redhead.

To the blonde he says, "I'm the primer minister of Canada. How much would it cost me to spend some time with you?"

The blonde replies, "$200."

Harper asks the brunette the same question. Her reply is "$100."

He then asks the redhead. Her reply: "Mr. Prime Minister, if you can get my skirt up as high as my taxes, my panties as low as my wages, get that thing of yours as hard as the times we are living in and keep it rising like the price of gas, keep me warmer than it is in my apartment and screw me the way you have the auto retirees of Canada, then it isn't going to cost you a damn cent!"

> **Q:** What's the difference between the Québec economy and the *Titanic*?
>
> **A:** There were some survivors from the *Titanic*.

Special Alert from the Federal Government

The Supreme Court has ruled that there cannot be a Nativity Scene in Ottawa this Christmas season. This isn't for any religious reason; they simply have not been able to find three wise men and a virgin in the nation's capital. There is no problem, however, to find enough asses to fill the stable.

David MacLennan

David MacLennan is a writer and photographer. He earned his BA in English literature from McGill University and his graduate diploma in journalism from Concordia University. He has been collecting jokes of various genres for some time and has written six other joke books.